THE FIFTY BILLION DOLLAR DRAIN

THE FIFTY BILLION DOLLAR DRAIN

Alcohol, Drugs and the High Cost of Insurance

by
John Krizay
with
Edward J. Carels

CareInstitute
Irvine, California

Library of Congress Catalog No. 86-071468 ISBN 0-917877-01-2
Requests for additional copies should be addressed to
CareInstitute, in care of
CompCare Publications
P.O. Box 27777
Minneapolis, Minnesota 55427

Contents

Foreword

In recent years, significant strides have been made in giving drug and alcohol abuse higher visibility, in establishing treatment and payment modalities, and in research. An increasing number of persons appreciate that addiction is an illness, more and more employers are paying for corrective services through the fringe benefits structure, and research has moved aggressively from the psychosocial to the basic processes of neurobiology. The associated behavioral research continues to focus on the societal problems. What information we have on the economic impact of substance abuse is highly fragmented.

Last year, CareInstitute commissioned John Krizay to do a preliminary study of the impact of drug and alcohol abuse on the cost of insurance in America. Krizay has pulled together a rich variety of impressive data and demonstrated that substance abuse has a major impact on the costs of life insurance, worker's compensation, health, fire, and property insurance. The overall results are staggering. Krizay estimates that the abuse of drugs and alcohol raises insurance costs by at least $50 billion annually. This figure alone should stimulate further study and heighten public interest. The author would be the first to support the need for additional facts.

Most of us who have been in the health insurance and prepayment business are accustomed to thinking of the impact of the heavy problem drinker on health premiums or rates, but clearly, the impact is far broader than that. As stunning as $50 billion is, the amount is probably low even after conceding a rather narrow construction of who an abuser is and what the impact of drugs and alcohol is on productivity and ability to cope. And, of course, insurance costs are only part of the problem, which the author points out. When quality of life is taken into account, the impact is far more devastating.

Under the circumstances, it is hard to understand why drug and alcohol abuse remain so far underground and hard to reach. It is somewhat reminiscent of the VD issue before World

War II, when many knew that venereal disease was a genuine threat, but few would talk about it. When, during that war, it was brought into the open and identified as a disease, not a penalty, it began to yield to public health measures.

Currently, most physicians are not equipped to deal adequately with drug and alcohol abuse. In fact, many aggravate the problem by prescribing tranquilizers to overcome patient anxiety, with the result that they contribute inadvertently to multiple drug abuse. Also, root causes at home or work may be lightly passed over. Not all employers have been willing to recognize the need for diagnosis and treatment, and therefore for adequate benefits. Not all hospitals have established the necessary expertise to deal with the stream of chemically dependent persons who present themselves at the emergency room, often under other guises. Collectively, we seem as a society to have an inexplicable tendency to divorce causes from outcomes.

It should be no surprise that the drunk is often portrayed dramatically as a tragic or comical figure. Yet, in real life, innocent people die every day from accidents or fires caused by drunks. The relationship of inebriation to tragedy is often not made in the dramas and comedies we watch on television.

It's time for such lack of public sophistication to stop. Recently, Governor Richard Thornburg of Pennsylvania signed into law legislation which requires health underwriters to cover alcoholism treatment. Carriers will rebel against this approach. Mandated benefits are seen as indirect taxation. Perhaps they are, but possibly employers, hospitals, and physicians need a "two by four" to understand what is at stake.

Some persons persist in the belief that the abuser is weak and that strong resolve is the answer. An attitude of "let him or her suffer" prevails. Possibly, the most important contribution Krizay has made is to point out that lack of concerted action is costly, very costly, and that costs are being borne by all of us, partly through insurance. He has given the hardhearted conservative a reason to act. This force, joined with the behavioral and clinical, may be just the added ingredient we need.

The Fifty Billion Dollar Drain deserves the full attention of legislators, employers, insurance executives, and professionals alike.

Walter McNerney
Professor of Health Policy
Northwestern University

Preface

There has been increasing concern about the impact of drug and alcohol abuse on our society in recent years. A Gallup Poll, sponsored by CareInstitute in 1983, showed that 33 percent of the families in America were adversely affected by alcohol abuse. Scandal after scandal has rocked the sports, entertainment, and business worlds. One cannot pick up a newspaper today without some reference to the insidious intrusion that mind-altering chemicals of all sorts are making on our lives. Drugs and alcohol have become a routine part of adolescent school activity. Not long ago, drugs like heroin, cocaine, and amphetamines were used only by those outside the mainstream of society. Today, the prevalence of drugs and alcohol is not limited by such distinctions. Substance abuse sweeps across all social, economic, race, and ethnic backgrounds.

This trend is accompanied by a number of other unexpected and unwanted social problems: crime, medical problems such as AIDS, industrial accidents, automobile crashes, deformed infants, divorce, spouse and child abuse, death by overdose, and so on the agonizing list goes. Exacerbating the existing trend is a serious new drug problem: designer drugs. Aspiring young chemists can now take an admixture of compounds and synthesize analogues to narcotics which are hundreds of times more potent, hard to detect, and often lethal. There are cases where only one use has led to Parkinson's disease or death. These chemicals can kill people in the best of health. The unexplained deaths of young athletes at the peak of their careers may be attributed to such synthetic compounds, or more commonly, to the unlimited access to hazardous substances on the streets and college campuses of America.

As we reviewed the available data on the economic impact of substance abuse, one thing became clear. This phenomenon led to a disease process for many users which, in turn, was costing this nation many billions of dollars in hidden expenses. Further, unlike other disease syndromes turned social problems, substance abuse was costing virtually all forms of insurance substantial sums of money. No other disease comes to mind which has the cumulative potential of causing or contributing to:

1. Early death (life insurance)
2. Automobile accidents (auto insurance)
3. Fire casualties (fire and home insurance)
4. Worker illness and injuries (worker's compensation)
5. Crime (home, auto, and property insurance)
6. Boating accidents, airline mishaps, train derailments and a host of other insurance claim (loss) events

A natural question arose: How much does the abuse and addiction to drugs and alcohol really cost the insurance industry? The answer was nowhere to be found. Further, like every facet of health care, chemical dependency treatment programs are beginning to experience the effects of well-intentioned and needed cost containment efforts.

The authors believe cost controls and proper utilization criteria are necessary to ensure a cost-efficient health system. We have worked on numerous cost-effectiveness projects through the years. We know that the true costs to insurance and, indeed, to society of chemical dependency is enormous. We remain concerned that this cost impact is not yet fully understood by the insurance industry, let alone the insurance-buying public.

A *Wall Street Journal* article on Friday, June 20, 1986, gives us a clue as to the future of drug abuse policy in America. According to a *Wall Street Journal* and NBC News poll, the public believes the drug problem is a higher priority than overhauling the tax system. Americans are justifiably concerned about drug abuse. The demand for drugs and alcohol is expanding. The supply appears unlimited.

Treatment providers are working to reduce the substance abuse problem by helping the addicted to recover. While all of this is happening, cost containment programs are asking hard questions about treatment costs. Many people are still not insured for treatment; and those who are may be denied the help they need because of pressure to contain health care costs.

This book was written in the hope that new light would be shed on the cost of substance abuse to the insurance industry. We wanted to show the degree to which it pervades every aspect of American life. We further wanted to underscore how costly this problem is to all Americans. Lastly, we hoped to catalyze research on this issue. A major stimulus for this project was the fact that no information seemed to be available on the impact of substance abuse on the various forms of insurance. Ultimately, it is our hope that by documenting how drug and alcohol abuse contributes to the high cost of insurance, there will be greater interest in reducing this serious social, economic, and health problem.

About CareInstitute

CareInstitute is a non-profit, public service organization dedicated to research and education in the field of behavorial medicine. The mission of CareInstitute is to advance public and professional understanding of behavioral medicine problems and issues through educational programs, seminars and workshops; through professional monographs and publications; through health policy analysis, and through applied research. CareInstitute's founder, Comprehensive Care Corporation, is the nation's largest private provider of chemical dependency treatment services.

This study, the most recent CareInstitute publication, was commissioned to stimulate public awareness and industry interest in the impact of drug and alcohol abuse on the cost of insurance. It is hoped that the book will encourage further research into the tremendous economic burden that substance abuse imposes on the insured population in America. It is further hoped that policymakers, the insurance industry, and the American public will explore ways in which treatment for alcohol and drug dependence can be made available to all who need it, and thereby reduce the economic and health impact of addictive diseases on our nation.

Introduction

The insurance industry is one of America's favorite scapegoats. When costs rise (such as medical costs or the cost of auto repair) causing insurance premiums to rise, we tend to find fault with the insurer rather than the providers of the services. When insurance companies take steps to curtail the rising cost of insurance premiums by limiting what they will pay out in claims, the insurance industry is accused of failing to accept its traditional role of risk-taker.

Insurance is, in fact, a major household expense, and one we often tend to resent. Most of us pay in more than we ever collect. Yet, the risks of being without insurance are enormous, so we pay. In 1985, we paid about $424 billion for insurance—more than $140 a month for each man, woman, and child; more than $400 for each average American household. Or, to look it at by another measure, total insurance premiums in 1985 were equal to about one-half of all federal expenditures.

It is a common belief that insurance costs so much because insurance companies make enormous profits. This is an attitude abetted by the luxurious insurance company buildings that embellish the landscapes of our major cities. However, if we were to take a weighted average of all insurance lines, we would find that 75–80 percent of all insurance premiums are paid back in claims. Logic should tell us that if we want to find out why insurance is so expensive, it would be more productive to look at the percentage of insurance costs that represents claims than to look at the 20–25 percent that represents administration, overhead, and profit.

In the analysis described in the ensuing pages, we look at that portion of insurance claims which can be identified as related to alcohol and drug abuse. The objective is twofold: (1) to attempt to "translate" existing research into substance abuse involvement in accident, injury, death, illness, fire, and property damage into an approximation of the cost of these events paid by insurance; and (2) to stimulate further, more rigorous research on the role of substance abuse and insurance costs, suggesting possible avenues of research as appropriate.

The first of these objectives presents obvious problems since there has been no research specifically aimed at relating the use of alcohol or drugs to insurance claims. There exist, however, a number of credible studies of substance abuse involvement in events that are typically insured. To attain our first objective, then, the task was one of searching out these studies and relating them, to the extent possible, to events in the way that insurance covers them. This line of study, of course, can lay no claim to precision. What we attempt to achieve, rather is a "first approximation," trusting that future, more rigorous research will refine these estimates.

The author is confident, nonetheless, that his estimate, derived from a projection of existing studies onto the insurance scene, is a minimum estimate of substance abuse impact on insurance costs. This estimate is approximately $50 billion—a staggering sum by any standard. Yet, the methodology applied in arriving at this figure indicates that the true extent of alcohol and drug involvement in insurance loss is probably considerably larger. This is not to say that the insurance loss events that involve substance abuse in some way would not occur in the absence of drugs or alcohol. There is no way one could ever make such a claim. If lightning strikes and kills the "town drunk," it is an alcohol-related event, statistically speaking. In a sober state, he may or may not have had the good sense to come in out of the rain.

Nonetheless, there is ample evidence that people who are under the influence of alcohol or drugs are more prone to accidents, more likely to cause accidents injuring or killing others, more likely to do harm to themselves, more likely to suffer a number of illnesses, and more likely to live shorter lives.

In arriving at the $50 billion estimate, only studies that produced a specific level of incidence of drug- or alcohol-related losses were applied. Moreover, where several studies have been undertaken with a range of estimates, the lowest was taken each time. Because no studies of any credibility exist in a number of areas, particularly regarding the use of drugs, and because it is unlikely that the lowest incidence is, in every case, the correct one, it seems almost a certainty that $50 billion is a low estimate. It is for this reason that further research would seem worthwhile. Precise results would yield valuable information for insurance carriers, affecting insurance design. It could change attitudes and policy toward workplace rules, not only in factories but in offices, hospitals, and in public transportation. The range of activities that are insurable and affected by alcohol and drug consumption is far wider than generally recognized. In recent years, there has been a laudable emphasis on improving traffic safety and reducing drinking and drug use. Drunk driving is, indeed, a major source of insurance loss. But, many other events, such as fires, workplace accidents, and erratic work performance, most certainly are the result of substance abuse too. The frequency of substance abuse involvement in these events can only be guessed at given our current state of knowledge. Many of these events are touched on in the text that follows, and it is pointed out where gaps in our knowledge exist.

As mentioned previously, our second goal was to point the way for future research. In that regard, it may be noted that one aspect of this study was to examine potential sources of information with the intent of assisting and stimulating more study. Hospitals and police chiefs were polled and asked specific questions regarding record keeping. There were consultations with the National Fire Data Center, with the Insurance Information Institute, American Council on Life Insurance, and with the National Institute for Highway Safety, among others. Regrettably, none of these sources is likely to yield the kind of information needed to determine the impact of substance abuse on insurance. Police, typically, understate substance abuse involvement, recording only the most obvious cases. Fire reporting, which asks for such information, is not likely to produce accurate data because alcohol or drug involvement is usually not immediately evident at the scene of a fire. Of all of these sources, the hospital is probably the most promising. Most major insurance claims involve some kind of medical intervention. Also, hospitals have facilities for precise testing, and records are generally meticulously maintained. At the same time, it has to be recognized that presence of drugs is only noted when the patient shows such presence. If an event was caused by an inebriated person, there may be additional victims who show no presence of drugs or alcohol. Yet, they too are victims of substance abuse. Still, rigorous investigation, using hospital admissions as a starting point, and proceeding from there to an investigation of other damage to property or individuals and related lawsuits, etc., could be productive. And, of course, expensive!

It is also conceivable that arrangements could be made with insurance carriers to select, randomly, a number of claims of various types (treated as sample strata) which could be investigated to determine the extent of loss related to substance abuse involvement. It is evident that this line of investigation would also be time consuming and very costly.

Beyond these possibilities for deeper and more rigorous research, it is hoped that continued research of specific events such as those relied upon for this report, will be facilitated in greater number and oriented more toward estimating the full extent of loss where substance abuse involvement may not be immediately apparent. Insurance loss provides an excellent and dramatic measurement of the unwanted side effects of substance abuse that all those who purchase insurance share. Since most of us are insured in one or more ways, there is a community interest and responsibility to exert our influence to assure that losses compensated through this mechanism are not born of needless and irresponsible use of drugs or alcohol. Knowledge and awareness are the key elements in the exercise of this responsibility—elements that only research can provide.

1

The Cost of Insurance in the United States

There is a tendency to believe that insurance costs are so high because insurance companies are either extravagant, inefficient, or extraordinarily profitable. The "exorbitant profit" thesis was most recently expressed by consumer advocate Ralph Nader and Robert Hunter, president of the National Insurance Consumer Organization (NICO). A year earlier, in celebrating "insurance freedom day" (the average American's last day of work to pay insurance premiums, which was February 14 in 1985), NICO focused on the inefficiency theme calling the insurance system "a monument to inefficiency."

Mr. Nader is not the first to cite huge profits as a source of high and ever-increasing insurance rates. The most important source of the high cost of insurance, however, is not to be found in profits or inefficiency but in the events triggering insurance payments. And underlying these events one frequently finds irresponsible behavior by insured members, with alcohol and drug abuse a major factor. Any level of "excess" profits or administrative inefficiency one may find in the insurance industry pales in comparison to the enormous cost caused by substance abuse-related events.

In the ensuing pages we can identify from credible studies, some $50 billion in insurance costs arising out of events where substance abuse was involved. And, it is a certainty that the true extent of alcohol- and drug-related insurance losses is considerably higher than $50 billion. This is because substance abuse is often not recorded and often not even detected in accidents, illness, death, or property damage events.

Insurance does absorb a large share of our incomes. Total insurance premiums paid in this country equal approximately 8 percent of our Gross National Product—a far larger proportion than that paid by the citizens of any other country. If payments for all types of insurance premiums were evenly divided among all Americans, each one of us—every man, woman, and child—would have paid $147 each month in 1985 for insurance. Or, to express it in terms of households, each American household would have paid $407 each month for insurance. On average, then, Americans spent more for insurance in 1985 than they spent in grocery stores (where the average household spent about $280 per month.)

Where the insurance dollar goes, or, more specifically, how alcohol and drug abuse contribute to the high cost of insurance in the United States, is the theme of this book. To understand this, however, it is first necessary to understand something about what insurance is and how it works.

Insurance is simply a form of "risk sharing"; a pooling of money by those who face some risk of loss, but who cannot predict on whom the misfortune will fall. While forms of risk sharing can be traced back as far as 4000 B. C., the modern form of insurance probably had its origins among the merchants of Venice at the dawn of the 15th century. Noting that, at each sailing, a fairly predictable number of ships succumbed to the perils of nature, the merchants created a fund from which the victim of the lost cargo would be compensated. From that simple beginning, the concept of insurance has spread to offer protection against every conceivable type of risk. The concept has changed little, but the form has changed drastically. While the merchants of Venice knew each other and the ship captains, members of an insured group today are probably not personally acquainted with their fellow insureds. More importantly, unlike the Venetians who sought to protect themselves against loss occasioned by Acts of Nature, today's insureds are more likely to seek protection against loss occasioned by Acts of Man. The 15th century Venetian could exclude from his risk sharing group anyone whose behavior or lifestyle might increase the likelihood of loss. Today, contractual and legal arrangements often preclude eliminating the high risks from the insurance pool. Even if legal obstacles did not play a role, the size and diversity of the insured population and the complexity of insurance itself make it unlikely that any insurance carrier could successfully eliminate the high risks.

It is in this context that alcohol and drug abuse contribute so immensely to the high cost of insurance. In spite of its potential dangers and destructive consequences, substance abuse is often tolerated in our society. This is also an acceptance of excess such that "abuse" many not even be identified. Insurance carriers are also tolerant. Even in those cases where driving or working while intoxicated results in injury, death, or property loss, the culprit is not expected to compensate the general insurance pool for the claims paid as a result of his irresponsible act. It is this feature of insurance that is often ignored when one considers the impact of drug and alcohol abuse on insurance cost: insurance can provide protection against any kind of loss which the insured has suffered, provided he or she has not deliberately or through gross negligence caused the loss to occur. The negligence of others is of no consequence except in those rare instances where the insurance carrier, itself, seeks redress from the responsible party through a process known as subrogation.

The behavior of alcohol and drug abusers can trigger excess insurance costs in a number of ways, not always obvious at first glance. In *Alcohol in America: The Price We Pay*, Rashi Fein notes the excess use of medical services by alcoholics. Comparisons of utilization of health care services between treated and untreated alcoholics clearly demonstrate that treatment can and usually does reduce the demand for other medical care. The impact on health insurance, in this regard, is evident. Much attention has also been devoted to alcohol, drugs and automobile accidents, particularly those involving fatalities. Here, excess insurance costs occur when survivors collect life insurance, and when the damaged or demolished vehicles are repaired or replaced. Less has been written about other accidents —such as boating accidents (where nearly all fatalities are believed by authorities to be either alcohol- or drug-related), home accidents, accidents at work, fires, and losses due to crime or negligence.

According to the National Academy of Sciences, "injuries are *the* leading cause of death and disability in children and young adults" in the United States. And, according to the Academy, "alcoholic beverages are involved in a large proportion of *all* types of injuries, including workplace and intentional injuries." When such injuries affect the working-age population, insurance costs are particularly heavy both in payments under life insurance and in disability payments that may well extend over the balance of the worker's life.

The actual involvement of drugs and alcohol in events contributing to the cost of insurance is likely to be underestimated in reported data, perhaps by a very wide margin. It is frequently overlooked that the actions of substance abusers often cause injury to others who are not abusers or even users. Unfortunately (from the viewpoint of data collection and analysis), involvement of alcohol or drugs is likely to go unrecorded unless the blood levels or other body fluids of the injured party show a presence of these substances. The same can be said of property damage. Property losses occur in a number of ways where alcohol and drug over use may be the underlying but unrecorded cause of the event triggering the loss. Losses through robbery and burglary—major insurance losses—involve alcohol or drugs in the overwhelming number of cases, according to careful studies. But where the victim may be intoxicated, the data are unlikely to record substance abuse involvement.

In fact, many property losses that result from indiscriminate use of alcohol or drugs not only go unreported, they may even go unrecognized. Damage to equipment or machinery in the workplace, or of personal property, may never be statistically related to drugs or alcohol. Yet even casual observation tells us that such property losses occur and insurance claims for such relatively minor losses are never questioned. Beyond all these examples, the fact is that much is not known about the long-term consequences of chronic alcohol or drug abuse on human behavior, nor is it always possible to test for drug presence. However, it is known that chronic substance abuse affects both mind and body in ways likely to make the abuser more vulnerable to injury or illness.

In the following pages, the findings will be detailed of researchers and official data that reveal substance abuse involvement in events commonly covered by insurance. These are the identifiable incidents. They are by no means complete, but are illustrative, nonetheless, of the enormous waste in life, health, and property that contributes, perhaps more than anything else, to the high cost of insurance.

References and Sources of Data Used in Chapter 1

1. U.S. Bureau of Census, Department of Commerce, April 18, 1986.
2. "Insurance Facts," *Property and Casualty Fact Book*, Insurance Information Institute, 1985.
3. *Life Insurance Fact Book*, American Council of Life Insurance, 1985.
5. Social Security Bulletin Annual Statistical Supplement, 1985, U.S. Social Security Administration.
6. Fein, Rashi, *Alcohol in America: The Price We Pay.* Newport Beach: CareInstitute, 1984.
7. *Injury in America*, National Research Council, National Academy Press, Washington, D.C., 1985.

2

Life Insurance:
The Cost of the Shortened Life
Span of the Alcoholic and Drug User

Those who abuse alcohol and drugs are likely to live shorter than average lives. Their beneficiaries will collect life insurance payments "ahead of schedule," adding to the cost of life insurance for those who live to normal term. Estimating precisely how much is added to the cost of life insurance by the early deaths of substance abusers is extremely complex, but the known facts regarding their longevity suggest that in 1985, at least $3.7 billion in life insurance premiums can be attributed to premature alcohol- and drug-related deaths. Just how this figure was determined will be explained later in the chapter.

The tables appearing at the end of this chapter tell the story of the shortened life span of the drug and alcohol abuser and, in turn, provide a basis for estimating how the cost of life insurance is affected. (More on this later.) The last of these tables, Table V, is particularly revealing. In this table, the average age at death (or average life expectancy) of persons dying of alcohol- and drug-related diseases is compared with certain other causes of death. It will be noted that victims of each of the other causes have a life expectancy in excess of victims of alcohol-related causes. Yet, each of the other causes appears to arouse more public concern and to command more public support.

Leukemia is one such example. Not a major cause of death, it is feared nonetheless, perhaps because many children are victims of it. Yet, we note that the *average* age at death due to leukemia is estimated at 61.8 years—older than any alcohol-related disease.

Cardiac disease ("ischemic heart disease") is a far more common cause of death, and, perhaps, is a cause of so much concern precisely because it is so prevalent. More than one-half million Americans—about one-fourth of all deaths—are estimated to have succumbed to this ailment in 1985. But the average age at death is estimated at 73.4 years, approximating the national average life expectancy for all causes.

Victims of strokes, which accounted for 179,000 deaths in 1985, live even longer, to an average age of 76.1 years.

By contrast, those diseases directly related to alcohol (Table I), though claiming fewer lives, will bring an end to the life of the afflicted person at an average age of just 53.6 years. Those who die of diseases that are in part related to alcohol are likely to die at an average age of 61.5 years. And, those who die in accidents where alcohol is involved will die even younger—at an average age of 38.9 years. Drug-related deaths are estimated to occur at an average age of 38.1 years.

Conceptually, it is not difficult to understand why these premature deaths related to alcohol and drug abuse increase the cost of life insurance. Life insurance, in its simplest terms, is a type of savings account with the ultimate withdrawal to be made by a designated beneficiary at the termination of the life of the insured. Or, it may be written so that the insured will receive payment of the amount of the insurance if he or she lives to the end of a certain term. Even in this form of life insurance (either "term" or "endowment"), there is generally provision for payment of the amount of the insurance to a beneficiary should the insured die before the designated period.

The expected remaining years of life of the insured, then, form the basis for determining life insurance premiums. This factor is crucial to the calculation, whether the life insurance policy is written as an endowment or term policy or straight life. While life expectancy will vary from group to group (for example, women live longer than men), within each group the averages listed in tables of mortality are used to determine the premium. When an insured person dies at an age under the age predicted by the pertinent table of mortality, there is a net cost to the insureds who live to the expected age or beyond. Conversely, when a person lives beyond the expected age of termination, there is a net gain to all others in the insured group.

A simple example may illustrate the point. Suppose that in a group of ten persons, each person purchases a ten-year term policy valued at $1,000. Leaving aside loading cost (cost of administration and reserve set-aside), if all ten were predicted by the appropriate table of mortality to survive the entire ten years, the annual premium would be $100 for each insured person. However, if experience shows that one will die at the end of the fifth year, an annual premium of $100 will leave the insurance fund $500 short:

$$9 \times \$100 \times 10 \text{ years} = \$ 9,000$$
$$1 \times \$100 \times 5 \text{ years} = 500$$

Total collected	$ 9,500
Total benefits payable	$10,000

This result comes about because the beneficiaries of the person who dies prematurely collect the full amount of the insurance. The premium, therefore, must be set at $105.26 so that those living out the term of the policy will be paying $1,052.70 for $1,000 of protection, while the deceased will have paid only $526.35. Although no longer around to enjoy it, it may be said that the prematurely deceased "gained" $473.65.

We can use the same format to estimate the cost of alcohol- and drug-related deaths to life insurance. The process is explained in the following paragraphs for readers who are specifically interested in the calculations.

In making this estimate, we assume that variations in insurance design and age at the time insurance is purchased are roughly the same for those who die of alcohol- and drug-related diseases as for those who die of other causes. This is probably a reasonable assumption in any case. However, a precise estimate would require some knowledge of the numbers of people fitting under every table of mortality, insurance characteristics, and the kinds of insurance carried by all persons dying of alcohol- or drug-related causes compared to those same characteristics for persons dying of all other causes.

Using available data, we begin with the estimated total public expenditure for life insurance, exclusive of annuity considerations. Annuity policies present a different type of problem which is discussed later in this chapter. In any case, it is estimated, based on latest experience published by the American Council of Life Insurance, that total life insurance premium payments for 1985 amounted to $57.4 billion. Note that this is not the amount people received as benefits. Benefits amounted to about $43.7 billion. Part of the difference is applied toward the cost of administering the insurance programs: collecting premiums, paying claims, maintaining records, answering inquiries, etc. Another part is applied toward "reserves." Reserves are needed to assure that there will be sufficient funds to pay the claims of beneficiaries in the future. Since the population is growing and since incomes continue to rise (partly due to inflation and partly due to real gains), the value of insurance policies in force must *exceed* the value of those policies currently being liquidated. Current year's premiums, then, reflect this growth pattern and represent the ongoing cost of life insurance over the lifetime of existing members.

This one-year cost can be translated into an average cost per death by dividing $57.4 billion by the expected number of deaths in the same year. The estimated number of deaths for 1985 was 2,028,250. Of course, not all of these deaths were covered by life insurance. But neither were all of those who died of drug- or alcohol-related causes covered by insurance. As we stated above, we assume that the proportion of insureds in the general population approximates the proportion of insureds among alcohol- and drug-related deaths. If our assumption is correct, we can safely use the average insurance cost of all deaths in our calculation. The higher the average cost per death of the pure insured population will be offset by the smaller numbers of insureds in both the alcohol/drug and general populations, and the final cost will be approximately the same.

With this technical note behind us, we can proceed to explain our estimate of the share of life premiums we can attribute to alcohol- and drug-related deaths. A total of $57.4 billion in life premiums divided by 2,028,250 deaths averages out to $28,300 per death. In other words, using *average* figures, the insured population will have contributed $28,300 in 1985 for each death to meet the level of benefits desired by those who buy insurance.

Let us now examine accidental deaths. Alcohol-related deaths are listed in Table IV, and an estimate of drug-related accidental deaths is listed in Table III. Combined, we estimate approximately 66,000 accident fatalities (including homicides) where alcohol or drugs (or both) are a significant factor. (The basis of these estimates is explained in the footnotes to Tables III and IV.) The average age at death is estimated at 38.7 years—51.6% of an average life expectancy. This means that almost half (48.4%) of an average lifetime of premium payments for the alcohol- and drug-related accidental deaths will have to be assumed by the survivors among the insured population. To put it another way, the equivalent of an average premium payment for those who die accidentally will have to be paid 1.94 times by others to make up for the payments lost due to their premature deaths.

In the case of accidental death, there is an added cost to other insureds if the deceased was covered by a double indemnity clause (paying twice the insured amount in case of accidental death). Double indemnity coverage has become increasingly popular, and, for these calculations, we assume that one-half of all insureds have such coverage (a conservative estimate). With these parameters, we may calculate the added insurance cost of this group as follows:

	60,000	accidental deaths related to alcohol*
+	6,000	accidental deaths related to drug abuse*
	66,000	
×	1.5	adjustment for double indemnity
×	$28,300	average insurance cost per death
×	.94	percent of annual premium picked up by surviving insureds
=	$2,633,598,000	

* See Table V

The same formula can be applied to deaths due to disease. Combining deaths directly attributable to alcohol with those partially attributable to alcohol (Tables I & II):

	38,000	deaths
×	$28,300	average insurance cost per death
×	.31	factor at age 57.4
=	$333,374,000	

Finally, we add drug-related deaths other than accident fatalities, with an average age exactly one-half average life expectancy (Table III):

	4,142	deaths
×	$28,300	average insurance cost per death
×	1.0	
=	$117,218,600	

The above estimates add up to $3,084,182,600. However, these figures do not include payments to another important branch of the life insurance business: annuities. An annuity, in its simplest form, consists of the payment into a fund during the working years of a person's lifetime, to be repaid in installments at some future date. Such a policy may or may not provide for payments to continue to a designated beneficiary after the death of the annuitant. Or, the program may provide specifically for payment of the annuity to a beneficiary as a way of assuring that the designated beneficiary will have an income.

There are no data to indicate what share of all annuity considerations contain survivorship or death benefit clauses, although it is known that such arrangements are quite popular. For our calculations here, we assume that one-half of all annuity arrangements include some type of survivorship clause. The same model as above is used in calculating the added cost of alcohol- and drug-related deaths to annuity considerations.

Purchasers of annuities paid $35 billion in 1985. One-half of this amount ($17.5 billion) was paid to plans involving survivorship arrangements. Nationwide, this averages out to $17,256 per death (since we also consider only one-half of all deaths). The average age at time of death of *all* those dying of drug- or alcohol-related causes is 45.2 years. (We need not make separate calculations for accident and non-accident victims since annuities do not typically provide for double indemnity.) Hence:

	$17,256	
×	54,081	deaths (½ all alcohol- and drug-related deaths)
×	.66	share of premium picked up by surviving policy holders
=	$615,920,651	

To summarize the life insurance cost attributable to alcohol- and drug-related deaths:

Accidental deaths (alcohol & drugs)	$2,633,598,000
Deaths due to alcohol-related diseases	333,374,000
Deaths due to drug-related diseases	117,218,600
Annuity considerations (all causes)	615,920,651
TOTAL	$3,700,111,251

Thus, as stated earlier, alcohol and drug abuse contributed $3.7 billion to the cost of life insurance in America in 1985.

At the beginning of the chapter, we implied that this was a conservative estimate of the cost of life insurance attributable to alcohol and drugs. There are various reasons for believing that this is the case. First of all, ailments listed in Tables I and II are limited to those where it is well established that substance abuse is either a primary cause of death or a known major contributor to the course of disease causing death. But, it is likely that alcohol adversely affects the course of other diseases as well. For example, substance abuse is known to diminish the efficiency of the body immune system making abusers more susceptible to all diseases. (It has been noted, for example, that there is a high correlation between AIDS victims and intravenous drug use, leading to speculation that drug abuse may be a key factor in the spread of this disease.) However, research has yet to progress to a point where these effects can be attributed statistically to specific diseases.

A similar situation prevails with regard to accidental death. With the exception of automobile accidents and, to some extent, homicides, the presence of alcohol or drugs is reported only for the person causing the accident. If, however, the person under the influence of drugs or alcohol causes the death of others not under the influence, these latter fatalaties are unlikely to be recorded as alcohol- or drug-related.

Little data are available on drug-related deaths. The data that do exist suggest that drug-related deaths are less common than alcohol-related deaths. This may, in part, be a reporting phenomenon. Alcohol and drugs are often used simultaneously. However, because the presence of alcohol is more easily detected than the presence of drugs, only the alcohol might be recorded in the reports that form the source of statistics.

A completely reliable test for the presence of many drugs has yet to be developed. Moreover, hospitals usually test for drugs only when some obvious symptom suggests that drugs are involved. Of some 40 hospitals in major metropolitan areas polled in connection with this study, many stated that testing for drugs was performed only in "suspicious" cases, when overdose was indicated, or if the patient, himself, called attention to his drug use.

The drug-related death statistics that are available are deaths directly due to drug dependence or drug overdose, as compiled by the National Center for Health Statistics. Table III lists the incidence of these deaths along with an estimate of accident fatalities where drugs are believed to be involved. The latter statistic is a "guesstimate" but, by all indications, a conservative one. (See footnotes at the end of this chapter.) For this approximate calculation, the presence of drugs is estimated to have been a factor in fatal accidents where alcohol was not a factor in only 10 percent of the cases. Some sources suggest a much higher rate. A study of 489 fatally injured drivers and pedestrians in Ontario Province (Canada) by Cimbura et al, found that 26 percent tested positively for drugs other than alcohol.

Even data compiled by the National Center for Health Statistics (NCHS) on deaths directly related to alcohol (Table I) may be understated by a considerable margin. These are data drawn from death certificates which are supposed to define the cause of death as "the disease or injury which initiated the train of events leading *directly* to death." In some cases, these certificates are completed by physicians. However, in other cases, coroners, who may or may not have the necessary understanding of medicine to render such judgments, complete the death certificate. Moreover, the insidious, long-term consequences of substance abuse might not be considered "the disease which initiated the train of events leading directly to death." Further, other sources have estimated much higher incidences of direct alcohol-related deaths than the numbers appearing in Table I. Olson and Gerstein, in their "Alcohol in America" published by the respected National Research Council, assert that 30,000 Americans die each year of advanced cirrhosis (compared to under 9,000 in the NCHS "Vital Statistics" series) and that 10,000 die each year from alcohol-related overdoses. The National Research Council estimates the total of these two causes would more than double the incidence of *all* direct alcohol-related deaths. So, while we can identify alcohol- and drug-related deaths that contribute to nearly $4 billion in life insurance premiums, the true figure, if complete reporting were possible, might well be twice that amount.

Estimated substance abuse impact on life insurance premiums, 1985: $3.7 billion.

TABLE I

INCIDENCE AND AVERAGE AGE
OF DEATH DUE TO DISEASES
100% RELATED TO ALCOHOL

Disease	ICD-9 Code	Estimated Deaths,'85	Average Age At Death
Alcoholic Psychosis	291	470	55.8
Alcohol Dependence Syndrome	303	4,363	54.3
Alcohol Abuse	305	1,123	43.9
Alcoholic Cardiomyopathy	425.5	671	55.5
Alcoholic Gastritis	535.3	111	54.4
Alcoholic Fatty Liver	571	986	48.1
Acute Alcoholic Hepatitis	571.1	814	51.5
Alcoholic Cirrhosis	572.2	8,884	56.2
Alcoholic Liver Damage, Unspec.	571.3	1,848	49.7
Excess Blood/Alcohol Level	790.3	6	50.3
Accidental Poisoning—Alcohol	860	398	45.1
TOTAL		**19,674**	**53.6**

SOURCE: Vital Statistics of the United States, Vol. II, "Mortality," National Center for Health Statistics, Department of Health and Human Services.

TABLE II

INCIDENCE
AND AVERAGE AGE AT DEATH
DUE TO DISEASES *IN PART*
ASSOCIATED WITH ALCOHOL

Disease	ICD-9 Code	Estimated Total Deaths	Alcohol-Related Share	Average Age At Death
Malignancies of Lip, Oral Cavity and Pharynx	140-149	9,106	2,004	64.1
Malignancies of Stomach	150	8,131	4,472	65.1
Malignancies of Liver	151	15,383	1,538	69.5
Malignancies of Pancreas	155	2,598	328	63.9
Malignancies of Esophagus	157	22,327	8,260	68.4
Pulmonary Tuberculosis & Other Resp. T.B.	011-012	1,757	703	65.3
Pneumonia	480-486	48,852	1,178	74.3
TOTAL		108,154	18,483	
Average age at death all incidents				70.4
Average age at death, alcohol-related share				61.5

SOURCE: Vital Statistics of the United States, NCHS. (Alcohol-related share based on study by Research Triangle Institute, 1984.)

TABLE III

INCIDENCE
AND AVERAGE AGE AT DEATH
ATTRIBUTABLE TO DRUG ABUSE

Cause	ICD-9 Code	Estimated # Incidents	Average Age At Death
Drug Dependence	304	730	33.8
Drug Overdose	850-858	3,412	38.1
Drug-Related Accidents (Estimate)		6,000	38.7
TOTAL		**10,142**	**38.1**

SOURCE: Vital Statistics of the United States, National Council on Health Statistics (Drug Dependence and Drug Overdose). Estimate of drug-related accidents assumes accident fatalities where drugs (but not alcohol) equal approximately 10 percent of alcohol-related fatal accidents or about 5 percent of all accident fatalities involving persons 15 years or older. This estimate may seriously underestimate the true incidence. The basis for estimation is weak; however, isolated studies suggest a much higher rate at least insofar as motor vehicle fatal accidents are concerned. Cimbura et al, in a study of fatal victims of auto accidents in Ontario (Canada) found 12 percent tested positively for marijuana, 26 percent for all drugs other than alcohol. Fell and Terhune, examining injury victims, found 10 percent of all vicitims tested positively for drugs without the presence of alcohol. (See Chapter V.) Reeve reported 16 percent of 1,792 impaired drivers in a California study tested positively for THC (the active ingredient in marijuana), including 24 percent of those who had no alcohol presence.

All of these isolated reports suggest a much higher incidence of drug involvement in fatal accidents than the 5 percent suggested above. However, given the dearth of studies on this subject, it was thought prudent to discount the figures used in these limited studies, and the 5 percent rate was chosen.

TABLE IV

INCIDENCE AND AVERAGE AGE AT DEATH
DUE TO ACCIDENTS ASSOCIATED WITH ALCOHOL

Type of Accident*	Estimated # Deaths 1985	Average Age at Death
Motor Vehicle	28,000	33
Falls	10,760	55.6
Fires	1,500	38.3
Drownings	2,600	32
Homicides	17,000	38.4
TOTAL	**59,860**	**38.7**

*Suicides are not compensable under most life policies and are, hence, excluded from these calculations.

SOURCES: Motor Vehicle Accidents: National Accident Sampling System, Dept. of Transportation. The 1985 estimate is a projection of 25,000 alcohol-related motor vehicle fatalities in 1982, adjusted for increase in motor vehicle registrations.

Falls, Fires, Drownings, Homicides taken from National Safety Council "Accident Facts, 1983" adjusted to 1985 based on 1985 U. S. population. Estimates of alcohol involvement in total accident fatalities based on the following: Falls: Haberman & Baden, "Alcohol, Other Drugs and Violent Death,"N.Y.: Oxford University Press, 1978.(Also, Honkanen, R. et al, "The Role of Alcohol in Accidental Falls," *Journal of Studies in Alcohol*, Vol. 44, No. 2, 1983. Fires: Gomberg and Clark (see Chapter VI). Drownings: National Safety Council "Accident Facts" and Report of Chief Medical Examiner, North Carolina, 1977. (also Haberman & Baden, op cit) Homicides: Wolfgang, M., " Patterns in Criminal Homicide," Philadelphia, Univ. of Penna. Press, 1958. Also, Zuska, J. J., "Alcohol: The Violent Connection," Newsletter, Calif. Soc. for the Treatment of Alcoholism and Other Drug Dependencies, April, 1975.

TABLE V

COMPARISON TABLE
INCIDENCE AND AVERAGE AGE
AT DEATH OF ALCOHOL-
AND DRUG-RELATED DISEASES
AND ACCIDENTS AND
SELECTED OTHER CAUSES OF DEATH

Cause	Estimated # Incidents 1985	Average Age at Death
Diseases, 100% Alcohol-Related	19,674	53.6
Diseases, in part Alcohol-Related	18,483	61.5
Fatal Accidents, Alcohol-Related	59,860	38.7
Fatal Accidents, Drug-Related (Estimate)	6,000	38.7
Drug Abuse (Dependence & Overdose)	4,142	37.5
Total Alcohol/Drug	**108,159**	**45.2**
Leukemias	16,951	61.8
Ischemic Heart Disease, Strokes	179,700	76.1

References and Sources of Data Used in Chapter 2

1. U.S. Department of Health & Human Services, Public Health Service, National Center for Health Statistics, "Vital Statistics, Volume II, Parts A & B," 1979, and updates provided by staff.

2. National Safety Council, "Accident Facts," 1984 edition, and miscellaneous materials provided by National Safety Council Library.

3. Research Triangle Study, 1984 (unpublished).

4. *American Journal of Public Health*, December, 1980, Vol. 70, No. 12.

5. American Council of Life Insurance, "Life Insurance Fact Book, 1984" and supplementary information provided by staff.

6. U. S. Department of Health & Human Services, Public Health Service, Alcohol, Drug Abuse, and Mental Health Administration, *Alcohol World*, Volume 9, No. 4, 1985.

7. Cimbura, Warren, Bennett, Lucas, and Simpson, "Drugs detected in fatally injured drivers and pedestrians in the Province of Ontario," Traffic Injury Research Foundation of Canada, 1980.

8. Olson, S. in collaboration with Dean R. Gerstein, "Alcohol in America," National Research Council, National Academy Press, Washington, D.C., 1985.

3

Worker's Compensation Insurance: The Cost of Alcohol and Drugs in the Workplace

When we think of alcohol- or drug-related injuries or accidental deaths, we think immediately of automobile accidents. Certainly, the intoxicated driver has been the cause of far too many tragedies, particularly among the young. The intensive, nationwide publicity campaign calling attention to this phenomenon is certainly worthwhile. Drunk driving is a major problem and a major cause of the high cost of insurance as will be described in later chapters.

Less well publicized are non-vehicular injuries and accidental deaths occurring in the workplace, which also frequently involve abuse of alcohol and drugs. The extent of this involvement, however, is more difficult to measure and, hence, is not recognized as a problem of comparable seriousness. Nonetheless, a number of limited, unrelated studies arrive at broadly similar estimates of the incidence of substance abuse in work-related accidents. These studies suggest that this is a problem of significant magnitude.

Substance abuse in work-related accidents affects the cost of many forms of insurance: health, life, property, automobile, product liability, and worker's compensation. This chapter will focus on the latter.

Worker's compensation insurance is unique in the sense that employers are required by law to carry it in all but three states: New Jersey, South Carolina, and Texas. Even in these three states, most businesses provide the coverage because they would be liable for the employee's well-being in much the same way under common law. Providing coverage under worker's compensation limits the employer's risk of negligence suits.

"Worker's comp," as it is commonly called, provides for death benefits for dependents of employees killed in work-related accidents, as well as income loss protection and some medical and rehabilitation costs for injured employees. State laws and court rulings have resulted in a considerable broadening of the scope of worker's comp coverage in recent years, notably by going beyond a strict description of accident-related injuries to include work-related illnesses as well. The "asbestos" cases have attracted the most attention in this regard, but the broader definition has also been applied to mental illness.

The stress-related disorders, whether the symptoms are physiological or psychological, are examples of ailments that can be traced to the workplace. Precisely how alcoholism or drug addiction will be interpreted in this context is not yet clear. However, there have been cases of "job-related alcoholism" being considered compensable under worker's comp. Two varieties of such cases have emerged: (1) where the employee claimed to have become a problem drinker because his job required him to consume alcohol as part of his representational functions (e.g. sales, public relations); and (2) where the job was so stressful that the employee was "driven to drink" to escape the pressures of work. These are new developments in the domain of worker's comp, and it is not yet certain how widespread such claims may become.

Estimating the extent of alcohol and drug involvement in worker's comp claims is complicated by two other factors: (1) the dearth of information identifying accidents where substance abuse might be a factor; and (2) the extent of the liability of the employer when an accident occurs because of the actions of an employee "under the influence."

Most of the pertinent information on alcohol, drugs, and work-related accidents has been obtained from hospital emergency room and hospital admission records. A survey of hospitals in major cities and a sampling of smaller metropolitan areas conducted in connection with this study revealed that most hospitals do record the presence of alcohol in the victim when an accident case is brought in. Hospitals are less likely to test for, or record, drug presence. (See Chapter II.) The circumstances surrounding alcohol-related accidents are also frequently noted in hospital records so that it is sometimes possible to identify those that originate in the workplace. However, collection and analysis of such data have been sporadic, at best. (The National Institute on Alcohol Abuse and Alcoholism has undertaken a project in collaboration with Johns Hopkins University and the Center for Disease Control to establish an Alcohol-Related Injury Surveillance System. The project has just gotten underway, and no data have yet been recorded.)

The extent of the employer's liability, which must be established before there can be recovery under worker's comp, is a complicating factor in estimating insurance impact. This is because one cannot automatically assume that a workplace injury always results in a valid worker's comp claim. In litigation, courts generally rule that an employee should not be compensated for injuries if they occurred while he was intoxicated. However, this outcome would not hold in all circumstances. For example, if the employer knew that the employee was intoxicated and permitted him to work anyway, it is likely that the court would rule that any injury suffered by the employee would be compensable. This aspect is further complicated by the affirmative action requirements of the Vocation Rehabilitation Act of 1973 which apply to people with "impairments." As mentioned earlier in this chapter, alcoholism has already been considered to be an impairment for worker's comp purposes, and it is conceivable that drug addiction could be similarly considered.

Finally, it should be noted that few worker's comp claims are actually brought to litigation. As a result, compensation for work-related injuries is seldom denied, whether or not the employee was under the influence of alcohol or drugs at the time the injury occurred. It is estimated by the National Council on Compensation Insurance that only slightly more than 6 percent of all claims were contested by the insurance carrier from 1980 to 1984. Interestingly, over 25 percent of all mental illness claims were contested during this period.

From the employer's point of view, there is little inducement to precipitate expensive litigation in an attempt to prove that it was the employee's use of alcohol or drugs that caused the accident (unless the effort was related to a desire to get rid of that particular employee). Few employers want to risk the adverse publicity that could result from an employer vs. employee battle. The employer may reason that "insurance will pay for it anyway." And any impact on worker's comp premiums is likely to be indirect, a remote prospect at best, and not one likely to influence the employer's decision to certify benefit eligibility.*

From the insurance carrier's point of view, there is also little incentive to take such cases to court unless the amount sought in the worker's comp claim is extraordinary. For one thing, the cost of litigation may exceed the benefit payment. Secondly, although carriers cannot recoup for past losses, the claims level becomes part of the rate-making structure. As long as the trend in alcohol- or drug-related accidents does not suddenly move upward, any effect on the carrier's profits is likely to be transitory.

In total, some 11 million persons are injured and approximately 11,300 people die in the workplace each year,

---

* Since income loss is a major determinant of worker's comp benefits, payroll size is the most important element in rate-making. Frequency and severity of claims are also taken into account but on an industry-wide level, except for very large employers who are experience-rated.

according to the National Safety Council. It is estimated that about 7.2 million injuries and occupational disease cases wind up as worker's comp claims each year. Of those injured, 1.8 million are temporarily disabled and 70,000 suffer permanent disabilities. An estimated 11 percent of all claims that are the result of occupational disease arise out of mental stress. Mental stress claimants are generally younger than other worker's comp claimants with 59 percent of them under the age of 40. This means that income loss benefits will be paid for many years in the future, making this category of claimant an extremely costly one. No data are available to indicate to what extent alcohol or drugs are involved in these mental stress cases.

Employers paid an estimated $23.5 billion in worker's comp premiums in 1985, about 70 percent of which was paid to private insurers. The remaining 30 percent represents self-insured plans and state insurance funds.

Estimating the share of this cost attributable to alcohol and drugs requires a great deal of interpretation. Our estimates are based on figures that have been produced by a number of independent studies of alcohol involvement in workplace accidents. A recent monograph published by the prestigious National Academy of Sciences titled "Injury in America—A Continuing Public Health Problem," cites a 1973 study of emergency room patients by Thum, Wechsler, and Demone in which alcohol was detected in 16 percent of patients injured on the job. The figure is similar to an earlier study by Wechsler et al (1969) also involving emergency room patients. The National Safety Council, in an April, 1983 newsletter, "Church in Safety," estimated that up to 47 percent of non-fatal occupational injuries and 40 percent of fatal occupational accidents are alcohol-related. In an internal document, the Council cited a 1968 study in France (Surry) showing that 29 percent of all industrial accidents requiring hospitalization involved alcohol. All of these studies suggest a very high rate of alcohol involvement in work-related accidents. These rates may be somewhat understated because of multiple injury accidents discussed above. The ratio of accidents to injuries is not known because data are compiled on the basis of injuries rather than accident events. However, experts at the Occupational Safety and Health Administration in a telephone interview stated the opinion that multiple injury accidents account for about 5 percent of all workplace accidents.

If we assume that accident victims are seldom denied worker's comp benefits because they may have been "under the influence" at the time the accident occurred, it would be safe to estimate that at least 16–18 percent of the cost of worker's comp is attributable to alcohol-related accidents. This is the lowest percentage revealed in any of the studies of work-related accidents from emergency room records. The figure, then, could be much higher since we have no data on drug involvement nor any basis for guessing to what extent drug abuse may also be a factor.

If 16–18 percent is a reasonable estimate of alcohol-related worker's comp claims, then $3.75–$4.25 billion of the estimated $23.5 billion spent for worker's comp in 1985 may be attributed to alcohol. Some additional amount—which we have no means of estimating—must also be attributable to drug abuse.

While realizing that the estimate is based on a number of highly tenuous assumptions, there is good reason to believe that it is a conservative estimate. For one thing, no cost is added to the estimate to represent involvement of drugs. Secondly, the problem drinker or habitual drug user can suffer impaired judgment even though not intoxicated at the time an accident occurs. Thus, the involvement of abuse would escape detection in the kinds of studies cited above. An additional source of under-reporting arises out of the tendency to cover up for co-workers in intoxication incidents. The most likely explanation for this frequently observed, but rarely documented behavior is that nearly everyone has, at some point in life, experienced intoxication, and it is natural to feel that "but for the grace of God," it could be you. Finally, nothing is added for the new category of stress-related ailments even though this fast growing claims category could entail alcohol and drug abuse.

Many of the same problems of estimation are also to be found with respect to health insurance which, to some extent, is complemented by worker's comp. It is to this category of insurance, where substance abuse constitutes a much larger share of total costs, that we now turn.

Estimated substance abuse impact on worker's comp premiums, 1985: $4 billion.

TABLE I

ACCIDENTAL WORK DEATHS—1983

Industry Group	Deaths	Disabling Injuries
Agriculture	1,800	180,000
Mining, Quarrying	500	40,000
Construction	2,000	200,000
Manufacturing	1,200	330,000
Transportation & Public Utilities	1,300	140,000
Trade	1,200	350,000
Service	1,800	380,000
Government	1,500	280,000
ALL INDUSTRIES	11,300	1,900,000

SOURCE: National Safety Council, "Accident Facts, 1984 Edition."

TABLE II

DISTRIBUTION OF WORKER'S COMP CLAIMS
BY DEGREE OF SEVERITY
AND AVERAGE COST PER CLAIM
(Claims to Private Carriers and Selected
Competitive State Funds Only)

Injury Category	% All Claims	Average* Cost per Claim
Death	0.1	$112,700
Permanent Total Disability	0.06	237,500
Temporary Total Disability	18.7	2,400
Permanent Partial Major Disability	1.7	49,500
Permanent Partial Minor Disability	4.3	9,000
Minor/no disability	75.2	150
AVERAGE COST ALL CLAIMS		$2,030

*Adjusted to 1985 price levels using CPI.

SOURCE: National Council on Compensation Insurance

References and Sources of Data Used in Chapter 3

1. National Council on Compensation Insurance:
   Emotional Stress in the Workplace
   Analysis of Worker's Compensation Laws
   Ratemaking ... The Pricing of Worker's
   Compensation Insurance
   Countrywide Worker's Experience Including
       Certain Competitive State Funds,
       Ultimate Report (unpublished data)
2. National Safety Council, "Accident Facts," 1984.
3. Insurance Information Institute, "Insurance Review," May/June, 1985.
4. *Supervisory Management*, July, 1977, Zepke, B.E., "Employer Liability for Intoxicated Employees."
5. *The Journal Of Family Practice*, Vol. 8, No. 6, 1979, "Accidents as a Symptom of Alcohol Abuse."
6. Thum, D., Wechsler, H., and Demone, H.W., Jr., "Alcohol levels of emergency service patients injured in fights and assaults," *Criminology*, 10:487-497, 1973.
7. Wechsler, H., Kasey, E., Thum, D., and Demone, H.W., Jr., "Alcohol level in home accidents," *Public Health Reports*, 84: 1043-1050, 1969.
8. National Safety Council Inter-Office Correspondence.

4

Health Insurance:
The Impact of Alcohol and Drugs
on the Cost of Medicine

Nearly every form of insurance is related to health insurance to a greater or lesser degree. Payment of benefits for life insurance is, in most cases, triggered by death, which is usually preceded by an illness entailing medical costs. Worker's compensation involves injury which requires medical care. Auto accidents, fires, boating accidents, in fact nearly every incident that results in the payment of insurance claims will, more often than not, involve medical intervention of some kind.

It is not surprising, then, that health insurance is the largest of all insurance categories in terms of annual premiums paid. If one counts Medicare, the government-operated health insurance plan for the elderly, the total paid in premiums in 1985 was estimated to have exceeded $200 billion ($213 billion to be more precise, of which $71.5 is Medicare). Of this amount, about $185 billion was paid to providers of medical services (physicians, hospitals, etc.) and prescription drugs, and the remaining $28 billion covered the cost of administering the insurance programs.

A rich literature already exists describing the benefits of alcohol and drug abuse treatment to reduce the cost of health insurance. These studies reveal that treated alcoholics and drug abusers will consume fewer medical services of all types than those not treated. A long-term study of California state employees by Holder and Hallan showed that not only do treated alcoholics use medical services less than the non-treated alcoholics, but that the use of all medical services by the families of treated alcoholics also declines.

It is well established that abusers of alcohol and drugs are affected by other ailments and injuries much more frequently than non-abusers. A number of ailments for which alcohol and drug abusers are particularly vulnerable have been specifically identified, and the degree to which the abuse of these substances contributes to the onset and continuance of the diseases has been estimated. There have also been attempts, as mentioned in the previous two chapters, to identify the extent to which injuries are the result of substance abuse. Yet it is almost a certainty that these estimates understate the real impact of substance abuse on the total demand for medical services.

The problem of documentation and reporting has already been mentioned in the previous chapters. It has also been pointed out that the effect of the actions of the substance abuser on others is likely to be under-reported, if not unreported, as a substance abuse phenomenon, in many cases. In the previous chapters, we related this deficiency in reporting to injuries where a person under the influence of alcohol or drugs has committed an act injuring or killing others who were not under the influence. A more subtle form of under-reporting of this type also occurs in the case of non-injury ailments. As mentioned above, families of alcoholics who have undergone successful treatment tend to reduce their use of medical services. This suggests that the stress of living or sharing a life in any way with an alcoholic or drug abuser exacerbates symptoms or, indeed, may bring on diseases. Such a living situation may make a person more vulnerable, less attentive, less concerned about his or her personal care, and adds stress to the lives of all family members. There is little dispute that such a relationship exists, but quantification in terms of added utilization of medical services is difficult.

It is also believed that alcohol and drug abusers show signs of impairment of judgment, increasing their susceptibility to accident and injury, even when not intoxicated. This point is well articulated in the National Academy of Science publication "Injury in America: A Continuing Public Health Problem":

> Chronic use of alcoholic beverages interferes with normal body repair processes and is important in injury causation. It is now becoming evident that use of alcoholic beverages predisposes to more severe and extensive injury than would be experienced by nondrinkers given the same severity.

Here is a description of a category of injuries where prolonged alcohol and drug use is certainly involved but would rarely, if ever, be noted as alcohol- or drug-related in injury data.

Substance abuse is likely to go undetected in hospitals unless the condition leading to hospitalization is specifically related. In "The Prevalence of Alcoholism Among General Medical Patients in Large Municipal Hospitals," a paper presented to the National Drug Abuse Conference in Seattle in 1978, Maze, Feldman, and Julie found that the ICD-9 code assigned as the discharge diagnosis failed to note symptoms of alcoholism in as many as three-fourths of the cases noted by the Chief of Medicine. Either for insurance reasons (many health plans exclude alcohol treatment), or out of a reluctance to confront the patient with an alcohol problem, many doctors conveniently avoid use of this diagnostic designation in hospital records.

Detection of drug abuse is even more sporadic, stemming partly from the fact that drug use is often not as evident as the use of alcohol, which can often be detected by smell. The variety of drugs available to drug users also makes identification of the drug user difficult. While new and more effective methods of biochemical analysis of body fluids to determine the presence of drugs have been developed, it is unlikely that such tests would be ordered by physicians unless there was other evidence that drugs were directly implicated in the illness.

The high cost of drug testing is one problem. There are so many drugs—each with different properties—that can be abused, that multiple testing procedures are necessary to assure detection. Moreover, since many health problems related to drug abuse may be indirect and the result of long-term use—such as effects on the immune system which make the drug user more susceptible to other illnesses—testing for drug concentration in body fluids may not reveal a drug relationship in any case. Complicating the task of detection is the fact that drugs that are abused include legal drugs—many of which may have been prescribed—as well as illicit drugs. All of these factors add to the complexity of studying and pinpointing the effects of drug abuse on health and utilization of medical services.

Finally, the scientific effort has not yet proceeded to the point where the consequences of substance abuse on all aspects of physical and mental health can be determined with the kind of precision needed to make complete estimates. The National Institute of Alcohol Abuse and Alcoholism and the National Institute of Drug Abuse are presently engaged in a joint effort to promote further basic, applied, and clinical research into the effects of alcohol and drugs. These include the study of neurophysiological and neurochemical effects of alcohol and drugs on cellular mechanisms, protein function, and immune system functioning.

An estimate of the cost to health insurance of substance abuse can only be calculated with respect to those medical services where a direct, detectable relationship can be established. However, it is widely acknowledged that the medical consequences of alcohol and drug abuse undoubtedly range well beyond these specific ailments or injuries. And even in this effort, one must rely on studies of limited populations and on general estimates of involvement of alcohol and drugs. Many excellent studies have been undertaken in this regard. However, the populations studied have, generally, been small and the results—though all confirming a significant impact of alcohol and drugs on use of medical services—show wide variations. For example, the American Hospital Association, in a 1983 "Policy and Statement on Admission to General Hospitals of Patients with Alcohol and Other Drug Problems," stated that "alcohol and drugs. . .(are). . .contributing factors in as many as 50 percent of patients admitted to hospitals with other diagnoses." In the Summer, 1985 Edition of *Alcohol World*, the Alcohol, Drug Abuse, and Mental Health Administration estimated that alcohol was involved in 50 percent of motor vehicle accident injuries, 25 percent of fire injuries, 40 percent of falls, and 10-20 percent of aviation, marine, and railroad injuries. On a more specific level, MacArthur and Moore, writing in the *Journal of the American Medical Association*, reported 36 percent of burn victims with an "alcohol pre-disposing factor," while Lang and Mueller in a Wisconsin study found the incidence of alcohol in burn accidents to be 61 percent. Numerous other studies of various settings reveal a widely varying impact of drugs and alcohol (more commonly the latter) on injury and sickness. Even though the studies may vary, none show that the impact is anything less than substantial.

For our estimate of the involvement of alcohol and drugs as a factor in the cost of health insurance, we have taken those ailments and injuries unambiguously identified with alcohol and drug abuse and applied a conservative level of incidence in the computations. This calculation provides a *minimum* estimate of substance abuse in health care costs, of which insurance pays only a part. Details are presented in Tables I—IV, appearing at the end of this chapter. Substance abuse-related hospital days are estimated for various types of injuries and illnesses from studies published by the National Highway Traffic Safety Administration, The National Center for Health Statistics (National Hospital Discharge Survey), and the National Institute of Alcohol Abuse and Alcoholism. Other sources (e.g., National Academy of Sciences) are also used in estimating the frequency of substance abuse in certain injuries and Research Triangle estimates are used in estimating illness frequencies. Hospital days involving alcohol and drugs add up to approximately 10 percent of all hospital days at an estimated cost of $22.4 billion (including cost of surgery, other inpatient professional services, and ancillary charges). Of this amount, private insurance and Medicare paid 79 percent or $17.7 billion.*

Outpatient services were calculated in much the same way as the hospital costs. The estimated number of physician visits by diagnostic category were drawn from the National Ambulatory Care Survey. Approximately 4.5 percent of physician visits could be identified as involving problems related to substance abuse at a total cost of about $3.7 billion. Of this amount, about $2.1 billion was paid for by private insurance and Medicare. To these numbers are added minor amounts for drugs and medical sundries, nursing homes, transportation, etc. ($700 million), bringing the insurance payment total, i.e. both inpatient and outpatient, to $20.5 billion. (Of the $20.5 billion amount, inpatient costs were $17.7 billion and outpatient costs were $2.8 billion.) Adding 12 percent as the estimated cost of administration of health insurance (relatively low compared to the cost of administering other insurance lines) brings

*Total short-term hospital expenses, 1985, estimated at $145.1 billion; surgery, related inpatient professional, and ancillary expenses estimated at $75.1 billion. (Long-term hospital expenses — predominately for mental and tuberculosis facilities — are generally not covered by insurance and are therefore not included in the calculation.) The calculation was based on data from *Hospital Statistics*, American Hospital Association Annual, 1984; *Source Book of Health Insurance Data*, HIAA, 1984; and *Health Care Financing Review*, HCFA, Fall, 1985.

the total health insurance cost of alcohol and drug abuse in 1985 to $23 billion.

There is little doubt that the true figure is higher. Projecting the estimate published in the monumental work "The Economic Cost to Society of Alcohol and Drug Abuse and Mental Illness–1977" (Cruze, Harwood, Kristiansen, Collins, and Jones, October, 1981), one arrives at a total medical cost of substance abuse of about $36 billion, of which the insurance cost (including administrative costs) would be in the neighborhood of $31 billion. This, too, was a conservative estimate; in fact, it is the median of two estimates. (The higher of the two Cruze et al estimates, projected onto today's price levels, would bring the figure to around $50 billion.) For the purposes of our overall calculation, we take the median between the estimate taken from the Cruze et al study projected to 1985 price levels ($31 billion) and the figure arrived at by adding all the hospital days and physician visits ($23 billion), to arrive at a cost of $27 billion to health insurance premiums related to alcohol and drug abuse.

Estimated substance abuse impact on all health insurance premiums, 1985: $27 billion.

TABLE I

ESTIMATED INPATIENT UTILIZATION BY VICTIMS OF ALCOHOL AND/OR DRUG-RELATED MOTOR VEHICLE ACCIDENTS

Severity (Abbreviated Injury Scale)	Total Number of Injuries	% Hospital	% Alcohol	% Drugs*	Average Length of Stay (days)	Total Hosp. Days Alc/Drugs (000)
1. Minor	3,273,000	6.20	20	3	5.2	242.7
2. Moderate	452,000	41.9	20	3	9.9	431.2
3. Serious	200,000	74.1	36	4	11.3	670.0
4. Severe	34,900	100	36	4	16.9	235.9
5. Critical	11,600	100	36	4	100.	464.0

Total Hospital Days, Drug- or Alcohol-Related—Motor Vehicles   2,043.8

SOURCE: "The Economic Cost to Society of Motor Vehicle Accidents," U. S. Department of Transportation, National Highway Traffic Safety Administration, January, 1983.

*Weighted average of all drug-related injuries = approximately 10% of all injuries. This is consistent with Terhune & Fell, "The Role of Alcohol, Marijuana, and Other Drugs in Accidents of Injured Drivers," U. S. Dept. of Transportation, HS-5-01179, 1982. For this estimate, it is assumed that drug incidence is highest in the most serious injury categories.

TABLE II

NON-VEHICULAR INJURIES

Primary Diagnosis (w/ICD-9 Codes)		Total Discharges (000)	
800-829	Fractures	1,118	
846-847	Sprains & Strains	319	
850-854	Intracranial (e.g., skull fracture)	282	
870-904	Lacerations & Open Wounds	316	
800-998	Supplementary classification of external causes of injury not listed elsewhere	1,502	
TOTAL SHORT STAY HOSPITALS		3,537	
OTHER HOSPITALS		870	(proration)
Secondary Diagnosis			
Residual calculation based on National Academy of Science estimate that 1 in 8 hospital beds occupied by injury-related patients		1,342	
TOTAL INJURY-RELATED DISCHARGES		5,749	
ESTIMATED HOSPITAL DAYS (7.6 days short-stay hospital ALOS x 5,749)		43,692	
LESS: Hospital days due to Motor Vehicle Accidents		6,355	(From Table I- Total Injuries x % Hospital x ALOS)
NET HOSPITAL DAYS—NON-VEHICULAR		37,337	
SHARE ATTRIBUTABLE TO ALCOHOL & DRUGS		12,496*	

SOURCES: National Hospital Discharge Survey, NCHCS, Dept. of Health and Human Services (1983 data adjusted to 1985 population). National Academy of Sciences, "Injury in America."

*Equal to 33.4 percent of hospital days attributable to non-vehicular accident injuries. The figure is a residual calculation based on the estimate that 10 percent of all non-federal hospital days involve alcohol and drugs. The figure is consistent with estimates of alcohol- and drug-related injuries in studies cited in text.

TABLE III

HOSPITAL UTILIZATION BY PATIENTS
WITH ALCOHOL- AND DRUG-RELATED ILLNESSES

Disease Category (w/ICD-9 Code)		Hospital Days Related to Substance Abuse (000)
291	Alcoholic psychosis	329
303	Alcohol dependence syndrome	4,677
305	Alcohol abuse	645
571	Alcoholic liver diseases	1,007
292	Drug psychoses	98
304	Drug dependence	758
850-858	Accidental poisoning by drugs	1,586
140-149	Malignancy of lip, oral cavity & pharynx	133
150	Malignancy of esophagus	179
151	Malignancy of stomach	49
155	Liver, primary	20
157	Malignancy of pancreas	271
296	Affective psychoses	863
300	Neurotic disorders	134
011	Pulmonary tuberculosis	111
480-486	Pneumonia	176
456	Varicose veins of other sites	21
531	Gastric ulcers	14
536	Disorders of stomach function	2
532	Duodenal ulcer	39
533	Peptic ulcer	75
534	Gastrojejunal ulcer	1
535	Gastritis and duodenitis	46
577	Diseases of pancreas	481
427.3	Cardiac arrhythmias	20
240-246	Diseases of thyroid	71
250-259	Diseases of other endocrine glands	1,313
263	Nutritional deficiencies	97
274	Gout	10

TOTAL DAYS—ALCOHOL- & DRUG-RELATED   13,226.

SOURCES: National Ambulatory Care Survey, 1981; Research Triangle Study, 1984 (adjusted to 1985 population level).

TABLE IV

OUTPATIENT VISITS FOR DISEASES RELATED TO ALCOHOL & DRUGS

Disease Category (w/ICD-9 CODE)		Outpatient Visits Alcohol- & Drug- Related (000)
	All injuries except 850-858	26,225*
291	Alcoholic psychosis	30
303	Alcohol dependence syndrome	518
305	Alcohol abuse	111
571	Alcoholic liver diseases	492
295	Schizophrenic disorders	56
304	Drug dependence	161
850-858	Accidental poisoning by drugs	580
140-149	Malignancy of lip, oral cavity & pharynx	53
150	Malignancy of esophagus	31
151	Malignancy of stomach	21
155	Liver, primary	13
157	Malignancy of pancreas	16
296	Affective psychosis	268
306	Physiological malfunction arising from mental factors	569
011	Pulmonary tuberculosis	46
480-486	Pneumonia	59
456	Varicose veins of other sites	9.5
531	Gastric ulcers	6.4
536	Disorders of stomach function	6.4
532	Duodenal ulcer	30
533	Peptic ulcer	125
534	Gastrojejunal ulcer	1
535	Gastritis and duodenitis	74
577	Diseases of pancreas	109
427.3	Cardiac arrhythmias	21
240-246	Disease of thyroid	352
250-259	Diseases of other endocrine glands	356
263	Nutritional deficiencies	5.3
274	Gout	108
	TOTAL VISITS — Alcohol- and Drug-related	30,452.6

*Based on National Academy of Science estimate of 99 million injury-related physician contacts in 1980, adjusted for population increase to 1985 level. Assumes 25% alcohol/drug involvement.
SOURCES: National Ambulatory Care Survey, 1981 and Research Triangle Study, 1984.

References and Sources of Data Used in Chapter 4

1. "Final Report: Selected Measures of Economic Costs to Society of Alcohol and Drug Abuse and Mental Illness, 1977," Volume II: Technical Appendices. Cruze, A.M., Harwood, H.J., Kristiansen, P.L., Collins, J.J., Jones, D.C., October, 1981.
2. "A Study of Health Insurance Coverage for Alcoholism for California State Employees," Holder, H.D., Hallan, J.B., unpublished report to National Institute of Alcohol Abuse and Alcoholism, December, 1976.
3. "Alcohol Involvement in United States Traffic Accidents: Where It Is Changing," Fell, J.C., National Center For Statistics and Analysis, Ninth International Conference on Alcohol, Drugs and Traffic Safety, November, 1983.
4. "The Economic Cost to Society of Motor Vehicle Accidents," U. S. Department of Transportation, National Highway Traffic Safety Administration, January, 1983.
5. Data from Drug Abuse Warning Network (DAWN), National Institute on Drug Abuse, 1984-1985.
6. National Ambulatory Care Survey, 1981, National Center For Health Statistics.
7. National Discharge Survey, 1983, National Center for Health Statistics.
8. "Physicians Visits, Volume and Interval since Last Visit, United States, 1980," Series 10, No. 144, 1983, National Center for Health Statistics.
9. "Injury in America: A Continuing Public Health Problem," National Academy of Sciences, 1985.
10. Source Book of Health Insurance Data, Health Insurance Association of America, 1982, 1983.
11. *Journal of the American Medical Association*, 231: 259, 1975, "Epidemiology of Burns," MacArthur & Moore.
12. *Wisconsin Med*, 75-S-5-S6, 1976, "Ethanol Levels in Burn Patients," Lang, G.E. and Mueller, R.G.

13. *Criminology*, "Alcohol Levels of Emergency Service Patients Injured in Fights and Assaults," 10:487-497, 1973, Thum, D., Wechsler, H., and Demone, H.W.
14. *Special Report to Congress on Alcohol and Health*, U.S. Department of Health and Human Services, 1981.
15. *Journal of Studies on Alcohol*, Vol. 44, No. 2, 1983, Hokanen, et al.
16. "Drug Dependence and Alcoholism: The Prevalence of Alcoholism Among General Medical Patients in Large Municipal Hospitals," Maze, Feldman, & Julie, National Drug Abuse Conference, Seattle, 1978.
17. *Biomedical Issues*, Vol. 1., "Drug Dependence and Alcoholism," Maze, Julie, & Feldman, 1977.
18. *British Medical Journal*, August 25, 1979, "Alcoholism in the General Hospital," Jarman & Kellett.
19. *The Medical Journal of Australia*, 1978, "Prevalence of Alcoholism in a Sydney Teaching Hospital," Williams et al.
20. "Perspective—Blue Cross & Blue Shield," Winter, 1978. Accident Cases studied by Dr. William Maxwell.
21. *Alcoholism*, Jan-Feb. 1982, Foundation for Health Care Study of Hospital Patients in St. Paul, Minneapolis Area.
22. *Health and Society*, Vol. 58, No. 3, 1980 (Milbank Memorial Fund Quarterly), "Repeated Hospitalization for Same Disease: A Multiplier of National Health Costs," Zook, C.J., Savickis, S.F., Moore, F.D.
23. *Alcohol World*, Van Natta, P. and Aitken, S. S., "Chronic Liver Disease and Cirrhosis as Alcohol-Related Diagnoses," Epidemiologic Bulletin 7: Vol. 9, No. 4, 1985.
24. Olson, S. and Gerstein, D. R., "Alcohol in America," National Academy Press, Washington, D. C., 1985.

5

Auto Insurance: The Cost of Alcohol, Drugs, and Driving

The effect of alcohol and drugs on the cost of auto insurance would make for an interesting and revealing study in itself. It is not only that auto insurance is so expensive, or that it is the third largest category of insurance (measured by the value of premiums paid each year). It is more that the automobile has become, for most of us, a routine element of daily life—as ordinary as walking, as necessary, almost, as eating. The tragedies that occur in this most natural of American activities hit close to home, posing a personal threat and arousing our interest and concern.

Adding to our personal fears, the tragedies on the highways strike at youth in a manner more devastating than war, without any semblance of glory or patriotism. No disease nor any other category of activities causes so many deaths to members of the 15–24 age group.

An enormous property loss accrues to us each year—a loss we share on a more or less equal basis as an insured community of automobile and motor vehicle owners. (An estimated 92 percent of all drivers are insured.) More than 52 million motor vehicles are estimated to have been damaged in accidents in 1985 at an insurance cost exceeding $40 billion, including damage to light poles, guard rails, and other non-vehicular objects that happen to get in the way of an errant motor vehicle. Bodily injury, "pain and suffering," and other claims arising out of injuries to passengers and pedestrians add another $20 billion to the cost. These estimates are based on "The Economic Cost to Society of Motor Vehicle Accidents" published by the National Highway Traffic Safety Administration in 1980, and were adjusted to 1985, based on the increase in motor vehicle registrations.

More than half of all traffic fatalities, 38 percent of serious injury accidents, 20 percent of all injury accidents, and about 8.5 percent of non-injury accidents involve an excessive use of alcohol, according to the National Sampling System of the National Highway Traffic Safety Administration.

It is not surprising, then, that the role of alcohol in auto accidents has been given much greater attention than other alcohol- and drug-related events that add to insurance costs. Although a common activity, driving involves high speeds and delicate maneuvers that call for alertness, agility, and peak judgment—all senses particularly dulled by the consumption of alcohol and many drugs. "Mental timesharing"—the ability to divide attention among the multiple tasks required of a driver, particularly on occasions when danger lurks—is one of the critical elements of driving skill that is most likely to be hampered by excessive use of alcohol.

For most legal purposes, "excessive" use of alcohol, or driving under the influence, is defined as a blood alcohol concentration (BAC) of 10 percent or 0.10. For a typical 150 pound person, the consumption of five one-ounce drinks of 80-proof alcohol on an empty stomach in a period of one hour would result in a BAC level of 0.10. Consuming one additional ounce per hour thereafter would maintain or increase the state of intoxication. (A 12 ounce bottle of beer or a 4 ounce glass of wine contains as much alcohol as 1-1/2 ounces of whiskey.) It has been estimated that the average driver is six to seven times more likely to have an accident if driving when his BAC level is at 0.10 with this ratio increasing to 25 to 1 at a BAC level of 0.15. These correlations between BAC levels and degree of impairment to a person's physical and mental faculties used in activities such as driving, are well established. That significant impairment to one's driving ability only begins at a BAC level of 0.10, however, has been brought into question recently by the American Medical Association (AMA). In fact, in January, 1986, the AMA recommended that a BAC level of 0.05 should be adopted as the legal definition of driving under the influence. Studies show that even professional drivers display signs of impairment, such as misjudging ability to steer through a defined space, at BAC levels of 0.5 to 0.6.

A vast amount of data has been compiled regarding auto accidents and alcohol, which gives us a basis for estimating the extent to which insurance costs may be affected. The data, however, considers alcohol to have been a factor at BAC levels of 0.10 and above. If the AMA's position is correct, and a BAC of 0.05 is a more accurate indicator of significant driving impairment, then existing data substantially understate the extent of alcohol involvement in motor vehicle accidents.

Data regarding driving impairment attributable to drug use are scanty. As mentioned in the previous chapter, methodological problems constitute the major obstacle. There is, apparently, no reliable visual inspection that would suggest that a driver is under the influence of drugs nor any simple roadside test that can be readily administered.

Nor are the possible effects of drug use on driving ability well understood. For one thing, given the variety of chemical substances people are known to use and abuse— the Drug Abuse Warning Network lists 268 different substances mentioned in emergency room drug cases—a comprehensive and costly research effort would be needed to determine the effects of each drug. The illicit drugs that are the cause of major concern and are believed to significantly affect cognition, mood, or psychomotor functions are cannabis, cocaine, opiates, and hallucinogens such as lysergic acid diethylamide (LSD) and phencyclidine (PCP). It is at least technically possible to measure for the presence of these drugs in body fluids. However, few laboratories are able to measure and quantify the relatively low drug concentrations likely to be found in impaired drivers or other traffic accident victims. Moreover, even if concentrations of these drugs could be readily and accurately measured, it still would not be known whether driving ability had been significantly affected. Apparently, the degree of impairment caused by these drugs varies widely from one person to the next to a far greater extent than one finds among persons consuming alcohol. Indeed, levels of concentration causing impairment in one person may cause no discernible difference in another. Too little is known about the consequence of multiple drug use or the degree of impairment that may result from chronic use. However, it is believed that the chronic user may encounter serious impairment of various mental functions even when no concentrations of drugs are found in the body fluids. For all these reasons, data on drug use and traffic accidents are scarce.

Factors used in this chapter regarding drug involvement are based on a 1982 study of injured drivers by Terhune and Fell titled "The Role of Alcohol, Marijuana, and Other Drugs in the Accidents of Injured Drivers." The study was sponsored by the National Highway Traffic Safety Administration. The presence of frequently abused drugs such as THC, cocaine, and tranquilizers was tested by analyzing blood levels in injured drivers treated in emergency rooms. Consent of the injured parties was required for participation in the study. About 38 percent revealed presence of one or more substances, with alcohol being the most frequently observed (25 percent). Most often, non-alcoholic drugs were used in combination with alcohol; however, in about 10 percent of the cases, one non-alcoholic drug (marijuana, cocaine, or a tranquilizer) was detected either alone or in combination with one other non-alcoholic drug. Another 3 percent showed a presence of anti-convulsants or analgesics.

Since only those injured drivers who consented to the study were counted (approximately 30 percent refused), one might reason that the actual number may have been even higher. Moreover, we do not know how many of the injured who had no alcohol or drug presence were victims of drivers who were under the influence. Yet these were, in a real sense, alcohol- and drug-related accident cases as well.

Our estimate of auto insurance loss related to alcohol or drug use makes no attempt to impute any level of unrecorded but likely substance abuse involvement, such as non-intoxicated victims of intoxicated drivers or drug use that goes undetected because of testing deficiencies. Only the level of incidence found in various studies is used in these calculations. The first step in this process was one of projecting the number of vehicles likely to have been damaged in accidents in 1985. Applying standard trend line analysis to motor vehicle registrations for the years 1975 through 1983—the latest year for which figures are available—a vehicle registration level of 170 million is predicted. Then, using the formula described in the National Highway Traffic Safety Administration (NHTSA) publication "The Economic Cost to Society of Motor Vehicle Accidents," January, 1983, it is estimated that 52 million vehicles were damaged in accidents in 1985. Of these, 3.1 million accidents are estimated to have involved injuries, and 41,000 involved fatalities. Of the remaining 48.8 million accidents, 12 million were unreported* and 36.7 million were reported to some authority or insurance carrier or

*The number of unreported accidents was developed from NHTSA's "Evaluation of the Bumper Standard," and Driver Survey on Unreported and Low-damage Accidents Involving Bumpers," Westat, DOT-HS-805-838, November, 1980.

both. Only 21.1 million of these non-injury accidents resulted in insurance claims.

The second step involved arraying the estimated number of damaged vehicles involved in insurance claims not only by injury and non-injury but by severity of injury according to the National Highway Safety Administration Accident Injury Severity Index. This distribution by severity of injury was derived from the National Accident Sampling System, which also provided the basis for estimating the level of alcohol involvement in both injury and non-injury accidents. Drug involvement was added on the basis of Terhune & Fell, as explained in the footnote to Table I, Chapter IV.

The third step entailed the actual cost computation. Two methods were used. The first applied average damage cost data for each level of accident severity as developed by the National Highway Traffic Safety Administration in the study mentioned above. (See Table VI-3 of that document.) These property damage cost estimates were then adjusted to 1985 prices using the auto insurance component of the Consumer Price Index. Bodily injury claims (largely consisting of "pain and suffering" and paid under liability coverage) were also estimated based on the NHTSA study.

Finally, 40 percent was added to the level of benefit payments to represent the cost of administering automobile insurance (adjustment expenses, sales, administration, taxes, dividends or profit). This may seem high, but claims handling in auto insurance is extremely complex and costly, involving professional appraisals and expensive accident investigations. In any case, by the method described above, we arrive at the following estimates (including insurance administration):

Alcohol/drug-related property loss	$7.4 billion
Alcohol/drug-related bodily injury	3.0 billion
Total	$10.4 billion

The second method used is simply one of adjusting the most recent insurance figures (1983) for changes in price level and motor vehicle registrations and applying an average alcohol involvement rate as presented on page 5 of the National Sampling System Report of 1982 (13 percent of all accidents). To this was added 3.9 percent representing drug involvement—the weighted average of all accidents involving insurance claims (see Table I). Combined alcohol and drug incidence adds up to 16.9 percent of all insurance-related accidents. With these factors, we can make the estimate as follows:

1983 insurance premiums $47.8   billion
(including insurance administration)

+ Adjustment for increase in motor   2.4
   vehicle registrations 1983-85 (5%)

+ Adjustment for increase in
   insurance   9.6

premium rates 1983-85 (19%)

= Total adjusted premiums - 1985 $59.7 billion

Of which, 16.9 percent are alcohol/drug-related: $10.1 billion.

An amount representing fire and theft should be added to these figures. How drug and alcohol abuse affect fire and theft insurance is discussed more fully in the next chapter. However, losses due to fire and theft of motor vehicles are generally specific components of auto insurance.

The rate of auto theft has declined modestly in recent years. In 1983, the total was 1 theft per every 167 motor vehicles registered. In that year, over one million motor vehicles were reported stolen with a combined property value of $4 billion. Insurance claims for motor vehicle theft amounted to $1.8 billion in 1981. The modest decline in the theft-per-registered vehicle rate since 1981 appears to have been more than offset by an increase in registrations than offset by an increase in registrations and in the increase in the price of automobiles and trucks. Adjusting for these factors, the estimated claims level for 1985 would be $2.7 billion, to which insurance administration must be added, bringing the total insurance cost to $3.8 billion.

The most recent motor vehicle fire loss figures are for 1982 when it was reported that 443,000 motor vehicles were destroyed or partially destroyed by fire at a loss of approximately $600 million. Adjusting for price increases and increases in the number of motor vehicles in the population, we can estimate total insurance cost at about $900 million including administrative costs(assuming that 90% of the destroyed or damaged vehicles were insured). Adding this amount to our estimated insurance cost of motor vehicle thefts, brings our estimated total fire and theft insurance cost to $4.7 billion for the year 1985. How much of this amount is related to drug and alcohol abuse is very difficult to estimate. The National Institute on Alcohol Abuse and Alcoholism estimated that 25% of all fire-related injuries involve alcohol. (*Alcohol World*, Wummer, 1985). It is doubtful that such a large percentage of auto fires involve alcohol, however. As to substance abuse involvement in auto theft, estimates of those convicted of crimes who were under the influence of alcohol or drugs at the time they committed the crime range from 33 to 60%. And, there is no way of estimating how often auto theft occurs because the victim was intoxicated or under the influence of drugs. For the purpose of this study, the most conservative estimate of substance abuse involvement in theft is used, 33%, and $1.3 billion is added to our total cost of alcohol and drug related auto insurance costs. Nothing is added for motor vehicle fire losses since we have no basis for estimating the substance abuse relationship to these losses.

Estimated substance abuse impact on auto insurance premiums, 1985: $11.7 billion.

TABLE I

ESTIMATED NUMBER OF VEHICLES DAMAGED IN ACCIDENTS—1985 AND ESTIMATED COST OF REPAIR OR REPLACEMENT ATTRIBUTABLE TO ALCOHOL AND DRUGS

Accident Category	Total # Vehicles (000)	% Alcohol	% Drugs (000)	Total Alcohol & Drugs	Cost per Unit (000)	Total Cost Alcohol & Drugs
Total Non-injury Resulting in Insurance Claims:	21,090	8%	3%	2,309.0	$1,228	$ 1,883,359.0
Injury Claims:						
AIS-1	2,531	20%	8.5%	721.3	2,164	1,560,893.2
2	365	20%	15%	127.8	2,530	323,334.0
3	134	36%	20%	75.0	3.955	296,625.0
4	20.5	36%	20%	11.5	5,364	61,686.0
5	12.2	36%	20%	6.8	5,407	36,767.6
6	7.2	36%	20%	4.0	5,407	21,628.0
Fatalities	41.	46%	20%	27.1	5,407	146,529.7
TOTAL PROPERTY DAMAGE	24,200.9					$ 4,330,822.5
+Alcohol- and Drug-Related Bodily Injury Claims						$ 3,093,671.0*
TOTAL						$ 7,424,493.5
+Insurance Administration						$ 2,969,797.4
TOTAL SUBSTANCE ABUSE INVOLVEMENT						$10,394,290.9

*Estimated total bodily injury claims = 1,846,000 of which 481,805 involve alcohol or drugs (25 percent) at an average cost per bodily injury claim of $6,421. (From "Insurance Facts," adjusted to 1985.)

TABLE II

SUBSTANCE INCIDENCE RATES
(INCIDENCE OF DRUGS
OTHER THAN ALCOHOL IN ACCIDENTS)

Substances Detected	% Subjects w/presence of substance (Any combination)	% Subjects w/presence of one substance	% Subjects w/presence of substance combined with drug other than alcohol
THC (Marijuana)	9.5%	4%	4.6%
Tranquilizer	7.5%	4%	5.0%
Cocaine	2.0%	-	0.2%

SOURCE: Terhune, K.W. and Fell, J.C.; Paper presented at 25th Annual Conference of the American Association for Automotive Medicine, San Francisco, CA - October, 1981, revised, 1982.

TABLE III

CLAIMS DATA AND PREMIUMS WRITTEN
AUTOMOBILE INSURANCE, 1983

Liability Insurance:
    Private Passenger $23,343,939,000.
    Commercial   4,736,128,000.

Total Liability $28,080,067,000.

Physical Damage Insurance:
    Private Passenger $16,974,304,000.
    Commercial $ 2,773,199,000.

Total Physical Damage $19,747,503,000.
Total Premiums $47,827,570,000.

Average Claim, 1983: Property Damage $1,020.
                  Bodily Injury $5,699.

SOURCE: Insurance Facts, 1985

References and Sources of Data Used in Chapter 5

1. "Insurance Facts—1984-85 Property/Casualty Fact Book," Insurance Information Institute, New York.

2. "The Economic Cost to Society of Motor Vehicle Accidents," U.S. Department of Transportation, National Highway Traffic Safety Administration, January, 1983.

3. "Alcohol Involvement in United States Traffic Accidents: Where It Is Changing," Fell, J.C., National Center for Statistics and Analysis, 9th International Conference on Alcohol, Drugs, and Traffic Safety, November, 1983.

4. "The Role of Alcohol, Marijuana, and Other Drugs in the Accidents of Injured Drivers," Terhune, K.W. and Fell, J.C., National Center for Statistics and Analysis, October, 1981.

5. "National Accident Sampling System, 1982," U.S. Department of Transportation, National Highway Traffic Safety Administration, 1982.

6. "A Profile of Fatal Accidents Involving Alcohol," National Highway Traffic Safety Administration Technical Report, Department of Transportation, HS 802 711, September, 1977.

7. "Automobile Injuries Related to Drug Abuse: An Introduction to Some of the Basic Considerations in Prevention and Research," Haddon, William, M.D., 1983.

8. "Epidemiology of Road Accidents Involving Young Adults: Alcohol, Drugs, and Other Factors," *Drug and Alcohol Dependence,* 10:35-63, 1982.

9. "Drugs in Fatally Injured Young Male Drivers," Williams, A.F., Peat, M.A., Crinch, D.J., Wells, J.K., and Finkle, B.S.; *Public Health Reports,* 100:19-25, 1985.

10. *Journal of the American Medical Association,* January 24/31, 1986, Vol. 255, No. 4: 522-27.

6

Miscellaneous Insurance Lines: The Cost of Alcohol and Drugs to Other Forms of Insurance

A variety of insurance lines are sold to cover certain losses which are similar in many respects. Hence, we find fire losses covered by homeowner's, farm owner's, commercial/multiple peril, and general liability insurance of various designs, including insurance sold for the specific purpose of protection against fire loss. Auto insurance also may cover loss by fires. Damage due to boat accidents is covered by homeowner's policies as well as by marine insurance. Burglary and theft losses may be the subject of a specific line of coverage, or may be covered under homeowner's, or any number of commercial lines such as "Banker's Blanket Bond" or the so-called "3-D Policy" (comprehensive dishonesty, disappearance, and destruction policy). Personal liability is also covered in a number of ways including through malpractice insurance, commonly associated with doctors and lawyers. These coverages account for about 12 percent of the total premiums we have identified in this study (about $47 billion in 1985).

Unquestionably, drugs and alcohol are contributing factors in the losses covered by all of these lines. Their overlapping nature, however, makes it difficult to determine when and to what extent substance abuse is involved in loss-causing events in a specific line of insurance. These are losses which often occur within the confines of one's home or one's business, and involve personal affairs. Reporting frequently takes place hours, days, or weeks after the event itself. Police or medical personnel, who provide the bulk of reporting information on substance-related insurance losses, may not be involved.

Fires

Of all the events covered by the insurance lines discussed in this chapter, perhaps fire losses have been subjected to the most study. Some of these studies have focused on the role of alcohol as well as drugs as causal agents. These studies, however, have concentrated on fatal fires which comprise only a small share of all fires in any given year. Of over 2.5 million reported fires in 1982, only about 5,000 resulted in fatalities. These are, in most instances, the most destructive fires, but still constitute only a small part of the total property loss.

The Federal Emergency Management Agency (FEMA) devised the National Fire Incident Reporting System which is now being used in most states. This report is quite long and detailed and includes questions which invite the local fire department to note whether any injured parties were impaired by alcohol or drugs. Such questions, however, are hardly the major focus of the report. As one seasoned FEMA official put it, reporting whether those involved in a fire showed signs of intoxication or not is not uppermost in a fireman's mind at the time. Filling out reports is at best a nuisance, a task to be completed as quickly as possible.

Where fire fatalities are concerned, however, some well-designed and rigorously executed studies have been conducted. These have been sponsored by the highly respected Bureau of Standards (U. S. Department of Commerce), and while not nationwide, they are extensive enough to suggest general orders of magnitude of substance abuse involvement. The most dramatic findings in this series of studies were produced by Berl and Halpin and released as a publication of the Bureau of Standards under the title "Human Fatalities from Unwanted Fires," April, 1979. This study, conducted under a Bureau of Standards grant to the Johns Hopkins Applied Physics Lab, examined 463 fatal fires in the state of Maryland. The study was restricted to "rapid" fire fatalities, which are those where death occurred within six hours after exposure to fire. Alcohol involvement in these fires was astonishingly high. Blood alcohol levels in excess of 0.10 were found in 70 percent of fatalities in the 30-60 age group. Fifty percent of all fatalities above age 20 showed an alcohol level of above 0.10.

More modest findings were reported by Gomberg and Clark and by Hall and Heltzer in two other studies sponsored by the National Bureau of Standards. These companion studies examined 1,600 fire fatalities in 12 states.* The Hall-Heltzer report, "Civilian Residential Fire Fatality Rates: Six High-Rate States Versus Six Low-Rate States," August, 1983, focused mainly on reasons why some of these states had higher rates than others. The Gomberg-Clark study focused more extensively on fire causes and examined differences between rural and non-rural areas. Alcohol and drug impairment were reported as the condition of the victim in approximately 20 percent of the cases with little variation between rural and non-rural areas (19.6 percent vs. 21.0 percent).

The difference between high-rate states and low-rate states was significant, and drug or alcohol impairment was found more frequently in high-rate states (24 percent vs. 19 percent). The studies commented little on these findings, and there was no speculation as to why the differences exist.

Substance abuse involvement in fires is frequently related to smoking as a causal agent. The scenario is a familiar one: the victim, intoxicated, falls asleep with a lighted cigarette or leaves a stove top or iron on. Awakened, engulfed in flames or smoke, his judgment is impaired and he cannot find his way to safety. How often this scenario is repeated when the inebriated person manages to escape has not been studied. Nor have there been any extensive

*The states included: Mississippi, Alabama, Arkansas, Tennessee, Georgia, Oklahoma (High-Rate states); Florida, Connecticut, Utah, Wisconsin, California, Delaware (Low-Rate states).

studies of injury-only fires, let alone non-injury fires (which make up about 98 percent of all fires). However, the limited studies referred to in Chapter IV (MacArthur & Moore; Lang & Mueller) citing alcohol involvement in 35-61 percent of burn victims suggests that substance abuse also plays a major role in non-fatal fires. As mentioned in the previous chapter, the National Institute of Alcohol Abuse and Alcoholism estimates alcohol involvement in 25 percent of all fire-related injuries. Since the most destructive fires typically involve fatalities or injuries, it is likely that as much as 20 percent of fire losses are alcohol- or drug-related.

Total property losses due to fires—excluding motor vehicles which were covered in the last chapter—are estimated to have amounted to about $6.5 billion in 1985. Of this amount, we estimate that 20 percent or $1.3 billion involved drugs or alcohol. Consistent with estimates in previous chapters, we add insurance administration expenses of $0.5 billion. Thus, a total of $1.8 billion of the cost of fire insurance can be related to substance abuse.

Recreational Boats

Property losses arising out of boating accidents do not add up to a very significant portion of property insurance losses. But boating is a rapidly growing recreational activity, and marine losses are certain to be a more significant factor in the insurance industry in the future. Boat ownership has become much more common in recent years, and the number of privately-owned boats increased from under 9 million in 1970 to over 13 million by 1982.

One of the most relaxing of all recreational activities, boating may also encourage the casting aside of restraint in drinking behavior. Consumption of alcohol or drugs is particularly hazardous on boats. Effects of alcohol are intensified by boat motion and by glare from the water so that impairment of motor functions and judgment is apt to occur more quickly than on land. And, this is an environment where errors of judgment can have disastrous consequences. One in six of the reported boating accidents resulted in fatalities in 1983—a ratio that has changed little in recent years.

Boating accidents involving property losses amounted to only $15.7 million in 1983—an insignificant figure in terms of total insurance costs. (Death and injury effects on life and health insurance were covered in earlier chapters.) There were 7,344 boating accidents and 1,241 fatalities reported in 1983. Of the fatal accidents, 163 were known to have involved alcohol or drugs.

However, it is a certainty that both the number of accidents and the number of alcohol-related fatalities have been under-reported, perhaps by a wide margin. U. S. Coast Guard Commander K. J. Morris, responding to a personal inquiry in connection with this study, wrote:

> The Coast Guard does not believe that the enclosed statistics represent all, or even most, alcohol-related accidents. Very few states use accident reporting forms which ask the investigator or operator about alcohol or drugs. . . . . The statistics represent only accidents which were reported by someone to the Coast Guard, usually through local law enforcement agencies. Many accidents are not reported. *We believe that nationally no more than ten percent of all non-fatal accidents are reported,* but we do receive reports on the great majority of fatal accidents.

Whatever the true rate, the insurance effect is not significant in any case since all property losses due to boating accidents make up only a small share of insurance losses. Nonetheless, the description serves to illustrate how frequently the influence of substance abuse on property damage, loss, accident, and even death is minimized or overlooked.

Crime

Property loss due to crime—robbery, burglary, larceny—is of far greater significance than many other lines of loss. While the role of alcohol and drugs in crime is generally recognized, the precise relationship is not always readily apparent. We frequently hear crime being associated with drug addiction. The simplistic perception is one of an addicted person turning to crime to support his or her habit. A not infrequent occurrence, to be sure, although the cause/effect relationship is certainly more complex. Whatever the underlying sociological or psychological factors that relate substance abuse to crime, it is clear that the two behavior modes frequently go hand-in-hand.

Joseph Califano, in his 1982 Report on Drug Abuse and Alcoholism, reported that 60 percent of all inmates in New York state were heroin addicts or alcoholics or both. NIAAA reported in 1981 that half of all inmates at Washington State's Women's Correctional Facility were under the influence of alcohol or drugs at the time of their crime. According to the Bureau of Justice Statistics of the U. S. Department of Justice, nearly 1/3 of all inmates of state prisons in 1979 admitted to "drinking very heavily" just before committing the crime for which they were incarcerated. Two of every five prisoners convicted of rape, burglary, or assault drank heavily in the year before going to jail. And, two out of five inmates with five or more convictions admitted to being heavy drinkers.

These reports confirm that criminals are heavy users of drugs and alcohol. It is often overlooked, however, that substance abuse on the part of the victim is frequently a contributing factor. The National Safety Council Report estimates that as many as 79 percent of assault victims had been under the influence of alcohol at the time they were victimized. Substance abuse can make people victims of crime in much the same way others become victims of fires.

Judgment is impaired, and one becomes careless about locking doors and windows, about where he or she may travel, and about the "company" they keep. An inebriated person is easy prey for the criminal.

The value of property loss due to crime is enormous. According to the National Safety Council, involvement of alcohol is as prevalent in crimes against property as in crimes against people. Excluding motor vehicle theft (discussed in the previous chapter), some 11 million incidents of robbery, larceny, and burglary were reported in 1983. Property loss exceeded $5 billion. (Federal Bureau of Investigation, "Crime in the United States, Annual.") But many crimes go unreported. The National Crime Survey, which estimates the number of unreported crimes, suggests that the actual number of incidents of robbery, larceny, and burglary may be over three times the reported incidence. And, one might speculate that a greater proportion of crimes where the victim may have been involved with drugs or alcohol would go unreported. Persons robbed while using illicit drugs would be less likely to report their own victimization, even if the loss were substantial.

Insurance claims data reporting losses under various lines that cover burglary and theft do not normally single out crime-related losses. However, the All-Industry Research Advisory Council (AIRAC) undertook a special survey to determine the extent of insurance property losses attributable to crime for the years 1979 and 1981. This study, detailed in a report completed in 1984, revealed that crime-related insurance losses had risen during this period at twice the rate of overall property and casualty losses. Non-motor vehicle insurance claims arising out of crime-related property losses amounted to $4 billion in 1981, according to that survey. Homeowner's insurance losses from crime amounted to $2.1 billion and Commercial Multiple Peril losses were $0.8 billion.

It is fair to speculate that the rate of increase in crime-related insurance losses has continued since 1981. This is because nominal values of property have risen and because greater awareness has lead to increased levels of coverage, as well as more diligence in submitting claims. The potential for continued growth in claims is certainly present.

For these estimates, we consider that only the reported crime rate forms the basis of insurance claims. The AIRAC estimate of $4 billion for the year 1981 is used as a base year. If property losses attributable to crime continued to increase at twice the rate of all property and casualty losses, as AIRAC indicated, the annual increase in losses attributable to this source would be 15 percent. On this basis, total crime-related property losses would have amounted to $7 billion in 1985. Adding 30 percent for the cost of insurance administration brings the total insurance cost (i.e. premium cost) of property losses due to crime to $9.1 billion.

All indications are that alcohol and drugs are involved in a major share of property losses related to crime. Substance abuse contributes to crime in those cases where the perpetrator is driven by the need to support a habit, or is given a false sense of bravado while under the influence. It is also a contributing factor when an intoxicated or drug impaired victim invites crime through negligence, carelessness, or impetuosity. If we take the lowest estimate of alcohol or drug involvement among inmates of prisons—1/3 estimated by the Bureau of Justice Statistics— we can estimate $3 billion in crime-related insurance costs with an alcohol or drug component. Yet, it is evident that this is a minimum estimate. This is not only the lowest alcohol/drug incidence detected among convicted criminals, it also ignores the role of substance abuse among victims (which the National Safety Council estimates at 79 percent). It also makes no allowance for unreported crimes, which, according to the National Crime Survey, may be three times the reported incidence.

Liability Insurance

The final element of insurance we examine is personal and business liability coverage. Claims paid under this line of insurance range from modest to astronomical. In California in 1983, the average award in product liability cases was $939,709; in medical malpractice cases the average award was $649,210. According to Jury Verdict Research, Inc., of the more than 1,100 verdicts on record involving an award of $1 million or more, product liability suits accounted for the largest share (over 25 percent). Medical malpractice awards were second highest in representation (about 18 percent).

Little is known about the role of substance abuse in these types of claims—claims that arise out of the misjudgment, carelessness, or fraudulent acts by oneself, one's family, or one's employees. Sources of such claims include improperly assembled equipment that injures someone or destroys property when put to use, material left in areas where unsuspecting persons may be injured by them, incorrect storage of dangerous substances in the workplace or at home, and errors and accidents in the practice of medicine, among other events. Negligence is the key factor in such claims.

How often substance abuse contributes to such negligence is unknown and data are scanty. There is evidence that claims are more likely to be successful and awarded in higher amounts if the defendant is charged with drinking or using drugs. Jury Verdict Research, Inc. found that the plaintiff recovery rate was 75 percent when the defendant was accused of alcohol or drug use and 51 percent when the plaintiff was so accused.

Among the various types of liability coverage, medical malpractice has attracted particular attention. Premium rates for this line of coverage continue to rise as successful lawsuits result in jackpot-sized, newsworthy awards. The effect of drugs and alcohol on malpractice incidents, however, has not been studied in any systematic way nor, for that matter, has it been widely discussed. There is little question, however, that substance abuse contributes to the incidents which ultimately lead to court action. Physicians, far from being immune to the ravages of drugs and alcohol, evidently have a higher rate of alcoholism and drug addiction than found in the general population. A report on "The Impaired Physician" presented to an American Medical Association conference in 1975, pointed out that between 1 and 2 percent of physicians had drug dependency problems severe enough to warrant their being reported to state licensure boards. An estimated 7–8 percent of all physicians were alcoholics, according to the AMA report. Joseph A. Pursch, M.D., in his book *Dear Doc* quotes David Smith, M.D., of The Haight-Ashbury Free Medical Clinic as saying that doctors are involved in drug use 4 to 6 times the national average rate, and that the use of cocaine, in particular, is on the rise.

Substance abuse is at the core of a significant number of liability suits. Because chemical dependency afflicts the population regardless of age, sex, ethnic background, or profession, it can be found at every level in every industry. From hospital staff members to attorneys to road workers, there are an alarming number of Americans who go to work each day impaired or intoxicated by drugs or alcohol.

While there has been no systematic recording of substance abuse involvement in liability claims, there are bits and pieces of information that give insights into how such incidents occur and how extensive they may be. Reports such as one appearing in the March 23, 198ɔ New York *Times* illustrate how chemical abuse can contribute to mega-buck claims. This particular story quoted National Transportation Safety Board Chairman James E. Burnett, Jr. as being critical of the way the Federal Railroad Administration handled two freight train accidents that occurred within ten days of each other in 1984, in Colorado and Wyoming, as well as a 1983 Louisiana freight train accident. All were believed to have involved alcohol and drugs, and damage was estimated in the millions.

Problem drinking among railroad workers was the subject of a study by University Research Corporation titled "Problem Drinking Among Railroad Workers: Extent, Impact, and Solutions." This study examined the drinking habits of workers of seven major railroads which had suffered 4,239 reported accidents in 1978 with a property loss of $65 million. Guesses as to the percentage of these accidents involving drugs and alcohol range from 1 to 25 percent. The study concluded that problem drinking was widespread among railroad workers, with the highest percentage of problem drinking found among operating personnel—where it is most dangerous.

Accidents and property loss involving aircraft also have a high incidence of alcohol and drug abuse. Although the commercial airlines adhere to strict rules regarding the drinking behavior of their flying personnel, this is evidently not the case with general aviation. The *New York Times* of May 8, 1984 reported a Federal Aviation Administration finding that 1 of every 10 private pilots killed in crashes had a positive blood alcohol level. Of 4,947 fatal air crashes during the period 1975 to 1981, 414 involved alcohol.

One could go on with anecdotal information demonstrating the consequences of chemical abuse in a variety of incidents involving property loss and liability claims. Consistent with the basis for estimates throughout this presentation, we cite only those incidents where drugs and alcohol have been identified as measurable factors by some credible source. No studies identifying measurable incidents to which liability insurance applies exist. Thus, for these calculations no substance abuse-related insurance cost is attributed to liability insurance. Yet, there is little dispute that some part—and perhaps a major part—of liability insurance losses involve the abuse of alcohol and drugs.

Premium costs for 1985 for *all* of the lines discussed in this chapter amounted to an estimated $45.5 billion. Our conservative estimate is that about $4.3 billion of that amount can be related to the abuse of alcohol and drugs as summarized below:

Activity	Estimated Insurance Premiums '85	Estimated Substance Abuse Impact on Premiums
Fire	$6.5 billion	$1.3 billion
Boating	insig.	insig.
Crime & Theft	$9.0 billion	$3.0 billion
Other	$30.5 billion	unknown
Total	$45.5 billion	$4.3 billion (identifiable)

References and Sources of Data Used in Chapter 6

1. "Rural and Non-rural Civilian Residential Fire Fatalities in Twelve States," Gomberg, A. and Clark, L.P., U. S. Department of Commerce, National Bureau of Standards, February, 1982.

2. "Civilian Residential Fire Fatality Rates: Six High-Rate States Versus Six Low-Rate States," Hall, John R., Jr., and Helzer, Susan G., U. S. Department of Commerce, National Bureau of Standards, August, 1983.

3. "Human Fatalities from Unwanted Fires," Berl, W.G. and Halpin, B., The Johns Hopkins University, Applied Physics Lab, April, 1979.

4. Federal Emergency Management Agency, National Fire Data Center.

5. All-Industry Research Advisory Council, Report on Crime and Insurance Costs, Oakbrook, Illinois, 1984.

6. Jury Verdict Research, Inc., Solon, Ohio. Especially, Special Research Report "Consumption of Alcohol and/or Drugs as an Issue," 1984.

7. Califano, J.A., *Drug Abuse and Alcoholism.* New York: Warner Books, 1982.

8. U.S. Department of Justice study reported in New York *Times*, January 31, 1983.

9. "Church in Safety," National Safety Council, March/April, 1983. (Reporting excerpts from 1978 and 1981 Special Reports to the U.S. Congress on Alcohol and Health, U.S. Department of Health and Human Services.)

10. Pursch, Joseph A., M.D., *Dear Doc.* Minneapolis: CompCare Publications, 1985.

11 "Lag in Rail Safety is Criticized," New York *Times*, March 23, 1985.

12. "Problem Drinking Among Railroad Workers: Extent, Impact, and Solutions," Manello, T.A. et al, University Research Corporation, 1979.

13. "Boating Statistics 1980–1983," and special analysis of current computer information provided by U.S. Coast Guard.

14. "Crime in the United States," Federal Bureau of Investigation, Annual Report, 1983.

15. "Criminal Victimization in the United States," Annual National Crime Survey, U. S. Bureau of Justice Statistics, 1983.

16. Insurance Information Institute, 110 William Street, New York Library, files.

17. *Alcohol World,* Summer, 1985, Vol. 9, No. 4, National Institute of Alcohol Abuse and Alcoholism.

7

Summary and Conclusions

In the preceding discussion, we outlined various ways in which alcohol and drug abuse contributed to the $424 billion Americans paid for insurance of all types in 1985. Based on credible studies, we have identified incidents where alcohol or drugs played a role, adding up to $50.7 billion in insurance losses.

**Impact of Drug and Alcohol Abuse
on Cost of Insurance**

Life Insurance	$3.7 billion
Worker's Compensation	4.0 billion
Health (incl. Medicare)	27.0 billion
Auto	11.7 billion
All Other Insurance Lines	4.3 billion
TOTAL	$50.7 billion

It is emphasized once again that the "identifiable" incidents may represent only a small part of the true extent of the involvement of drugs and alcohol in insurance claims. This is because there is no systematic recording of many events which are alcohol- or drug-related because there are practical limitations to readily detecting the presence of many drugs. In addition, much is not known, particularly about the long-term effects of drug use on motor ability, judgment, and the immune system. Evidence strongly suggests, however, that all of these functions are affected in ways that contribute to illness, accident and, hence, insurance loss.

What does insurance loss measure? It should be noted that insurance loss is not a measure of the "cost to society" of substance abuse—an approach used in many studies. The insurance loss we have identified here constitutes a measure of the waste that irresponsible drinking and drug-using behavior can cause. Since insurance, to a large extent, is a personal expense, this is a very personal measure of how much of our income is consumed to compensate for mistakes and tragedies that occur because of someone's misuse or abusive use of drugs and alcohol. As individuals, we would not likely countenance such a level of waste out of our personal, discretionary incomes. Collectively, should we be less concerned about contributing the same amount of money to the insurance pool?

No matter how we measure the cost of drug and alcohol abuse that we share as members of the insured population, it is unquestionably a major problem in the United States. How is society to deal with it? Alcohol abuse is not a new problem in our culture, and efforts to control or modify consumption of alcohol have a long but unimpressive history. Drug abuse is a more recent phenomenon in this country, and it may be premature to judge whether the current efforts combining legal sanctions and moral persuasion will eventually succeed.

In the long run, it may be that alcohol abuse will prove the more intractable of the two. Its longer history is indicative of the strength of the human craving for this substance. History also tells us that the dangers of excessive use of alcohol have been recognized for thousands of years. A 3,000 year old papyrus from ancient Egypt contains this warning:

> Make not thyself helpless drinking in the
> beer shop . . . falling down, thy limbs will
> be broken and no one will give thee a hand
> to help thee up.

It is clear that consumption of alcohol is not something that can be eliminated. But we should strive to minimize problem drinking and the damage it causes in human and property loss.

According to surveys of drinking habits conducted by the Rand Corporation, 5 percent of the population consumes half of all alcoholic beverages. These are people who consume 10 or more drinks per day. Another 10 percent consume 3 or more drinks per day. If we consider this group to be chronic, heavy drinkers, the chronic drinker problem is confined to a small part of the population.

Opening the avenues to treatment facilities probably constitutes the best hope of moderating the risks to self and society for alcohol and drug abusers. Effective drug and alcohol treatment is available in virtually every community. Treatment has been shown to be effective in reducing accidents in the workplace as well as in reducing the incidence of diseases caused by or related to alcoholism or drug addiction. The U. S. Office of Technology, for example, found after extensive study that more people improved after treatment than would occur by chance (i.e., with no treatment). Various studies indicate that about 2/3 of those treated maintain sobriety for at least 12–18 months. This is the maximum time it has been possible to systematically monitor alcohol patients, given the financial constraints on current research efforts. Prestigious establishments such as Kimberly-Clark, E. I. duPont de Nemours, and Illinois Bell have found alcohol treatment programs to be effective.

On a per capita, group basis, treatment is quite inexpensive even if one does not count the obvious offsets in reduced medical costs and decreased time and equipment loss in the workplace. Depending upon the age distribution of the insured group, its geographic location, and other relevant factors, complete treatment coverage can be as low as $5 per covered person per year. Yet, among medium and large size firms in the United States, about 1/3 of all employees have no coverage for this type of treatment whatsoever. Many of those who *are* covered have very limited coverage, often for detoxification only. Among the self-employed and employees of small firms, the percentage of those without coverage is no doubt much higher.

Substance abuse treatment may also benefit moderate drinkers who consume far less alcohol than the chronic alcoholic, but who may still be the cause of many accidents, injuring or killing themselves or others. Many teenagers involved in alcohol-related accidents probably fit this description.

Treatment aside, other aspects of public policy could also be modified to help combat this problem. Drunk driving laws, for example, could be emulated in the workplace where intoxication can be just as lethal as on the highways. The tendency for fellow workers, and sometimes labor unions as well, to "protect" workers under the influence might be mitigated if intoxication on-the-job were unlawful. It is ironic that OSHA (Occupational Safety and Health Administration) has been so conscientious in pursuing work safety rules but has ignored the much larger threat to safety imposed by irresponsible drinking habits. In fact, OSHA does not even seek or keep statistics on substance abuse-related accidents.

The cost of alcoholic beverages also influences the quantity of alcohol consumed. Alcohol consumption increased by 30 percent on a per capita basis from 1950 to 1980 as the real (i.e. constant dollar) price declined and incomes rose. This suggests that the demand for alcoholic beverages may be both price and income elastic. Alcoholic beverage taxes could be sharply increased, if this is the case, as one way of curtailing excessive drinking. Such a policy might be particularly effective in the case of teenage drinking. (This approach, of course, requires careful study since increasing the tax too much would only encourage illegal or "bootleg" production and sales.)

Finally, a somewhat different "educational" approach to the risks of excessive drinking might be tried. While vivid portrayals of terrible auto accidents dramatize the dangers, most people tend to think they will not be victims. Likewise, advertising the warning signs of alcoholism, while helpful to families of problem drinkers, does not address the potential danger of the person who only occasionally consumes alcohol in excess and would not be considered an alcoholic. Perhaps a program describing the early signs of intoxication would have a greater impact, particularly on teenage drinkers. Such a program could be carried out in schools.

The drug problem is somewhat different. Most drugs that are abused are illegal, and criminal penalties already exist for possession, use, and sale of these substances. The price users pay for these substances is high, and is driven even higher when supply levels drop.

Beyond educational programs and law enforcement, effective treatment programs also exist for drug abuse. However, even fewer health insurance plans cover drug abuse treatment than treatment for alcoholism. According to the Bureau of Labor Statistics, only 61 percent of full-time employees of medium and large size establishments have such coverage. Again, it appears that much of this coverage is limited to detoxification. It would be in the interest of public policy to require treatment for drug abuse as well as alcoholism treatment as an ingredient of health insurance plans.

Deeper research into insurance costs is a worthy objective both as a way of dramatizing the extent of the problem, and as a way of bringing it to the attention of large employers who are purchasers of multiple insurance lines. There is frequently little coordination among the managers in large establishments who have the responsibility of purchasing insurance against the myriad risks that their firms encounter. Consequently, the benefits of covering alcohol and drug treatment in terms of the cost of worker's compensation insurance, product liability, fire and other lines are not likely to be considered.

The insurance industry, itself, might find marketing value in taking into account a company's policy toward drugs and alcohol in rate making. Since substance abuse obviously plays a significant role in numerous events that trigger insurance claims—from worker's comp to product liability—the forward-looking company with an active employee assistance program and coverage of substance abuse treatment in its health plan would seem to be a lower risk than a company that ignores the problem.

The relatively small amounts we would spend as a society to make substance abuse treatment universally available would contribute to substantial savings in insurance costs alone. If 10 percent of the *identifiable* substance abuse-related insurance losses could be eliminated, the insured public would realize a savings of $5 billion a year. Five billion dollars is, for example, what has been proposed as the annual cost to equip automobiles with air bags. Like substance abuse, the air bag issue is, in reality, a health issue. According to a recent NHTSA Status Report, it is estimated that air bags will cost about $500 each and that between 5,200 and 11,100 lives will be saved annually *once all passenger vehicles are so equipped.* At a cost of $500 per vehicle, if 10 million new vehicles are manufactured annually, Americans will be paying $5 billion every year to save, once all cars are so equipped, 5,200 to 11,100 lives. Thus, air bags will cost $450,000 to $1 million per life saved. It is proper to argue that value cannot be placed on a life saved; yet it is ironic that we are willing to spend so little on treatment of a disease that costs, by most conservative estimate, in excess of 100,000 lives per year.

There is no doubt that efforts to promote public awareness of the dangers and risks of alcohol and drug abuse have gained momentum in recent years. Recognition that addiction to these substances is a disease has encouraged victims to seek professional help. Acceptance has been encouraged by the public statements of well-known personalities who have, themselves, overcome the problem with professional support. There is unquestionably less of a stigma to seeking treatment than might have been the case even a decade ago. There has been progress in other areas as well, such as in traffic safety (more stringent drunk driving laws), and in reversal of laws in some states that had earlier lowered the drinking age below 21. Still, a full understanding of the impact of substance abuse on long-term personal health, on accidents in factories, offices, and public transportation— and even in operating rooms and court rooms—remains to be accomplished. Effective solutions can only come with more complete knowledge of the magnitude of the problem, and this can only be attained through broader and more rigorous research. Federal funding of research devoted to alcohol and drug abuse currently amounts to about $150 million—about 3 percent of the estimated insurance loss attributable to substance abuse in this presentation. A very modest addition to current research levels would permit a long-term, systematic analysis of the involvement of drugs and alcohol in events typically covered by insurance. Such research would do more than yield a more precise measure of insurance loss; it should also provide information of value to insurance design, workplace rules, and to improving personal health and well-being. Given the apparent enormity of losses we are now experiencing, there is almost a certainty that a minor investment in research would yield rich returns.

References and Sources of Data Used in Chapter 7

1. Polich, J.M. and Orvis, B.R., "Alcohol Problems, Patterns, and Prevalence in the U.S. Air Force." Santa Monica: Rand Corporation, 1979.

2. Clark, W.B. and Midanik, L., National Survey. Social Research Group, University of California, Berkeley, 1980.

3. "The Effectiveness and Costs of Alcohol Treatment," Congressional Office of Technology, March, 1983. Health Technology Case Study 22.

4. Jones, K.R. and Vischi, T.R., "Impact of Alcohol, Drug Abuse, and Mental Health Treatment on Medical Care Utilization," *Supplement of Medical Care*, Vol. 17 No. 12, December 1979.

5. Statement of Burford W. Culpepper, M.D., Assistant Medical Director, E.I. duPont de Nemours. U.S. Senate Sub-Committee on Alcoholism and Drug Abuse, July 14, 1982.

6. "Employee Benefits in Medium and Large Firms, 1985," Bureau of Labor Statistics, U.S. Department of Labor, July, 1986.

7. Olson, Steve and Gerstein, D.R., *Alcohol in America*. National Academy Press, 1985.

8. "Status Report," Insurance Institute for Highway Safety, Vol. 18 No. 18, December, 1983.

About the Authors

John Krizay is a noted researcher, writer, and consultant on health economics. He was the research director of the 20th Century Fund "Study on Financing Medical Costs in the United States" and has also served as an instructor and professor of economics and medical economics. In 1974, Krizay received the Norman B. Welch, M.D. Award for "the outstanding contribution to the literature of medical economics." He has published several journal and newspaper articles on health and economic issues. During a long and distinguished career in the Foreign Service, Krizay achieved the rank of Minister-Counselor. Other government service includes senior positions at the Department of State, where he served as Director for Latin American Economic Policy and Director of the Office on Monetary Affairs. Krizay received a bachelor's degree in International Relations and Economics from George Washington University, and his master's degree in Economics from Yale.

Edward J. Carels, Ph.D., has extensive business experience in the health care field, and has held the positions of senior vice president of Comprehensive Care Corporation, assistant vice president for Blue Shield Association, and director of research for Health Care Management Systems, Inc. He also has clinical experience as a counselor of patients suffering from alcoholism. Carels was on the faculty of Northeastern Illinois University in the psychology department. Recent activities include serving as a consultant to the American Medical Association, American Psychiatric Association, the American College of Physicians, and the Office of Technology Assessment. The author of several books and papers, Carels has also given Congressional Testimony on a variety of health care topics. He holds a doctorate in Educational Psychology from Loyola University in Chicago, a bachelor's degree in Psychology from Rutgers University, and a master's degree in Experimental Psychology from Villanova University.